PRACTICAL HOUSEHOLD USES OF

SALT

D0111809

PRACTICAL HOUSEHOLD USES OF

SALT

HOME CURES, RECIPES, EVERYDAY HINTS AND TIPS

MARGARET BRIGGS

southwater

This edition is published by Southwater,
an imprint of Anness Publishing Ltd
Blaby Road
Wigston
Leicestershire LE18 4SE
info@anness.com

www.southwaterbooks.com;
www.annesspublishing.com

A CIP catalogue record for this book
is available from the British Library.

Publisher: Joanna Lorenz
Senior Editor: Felicity Forster
Cover Design: Nigel Partridge
Production Controller: Mai-Ling Collyer

PUBLISHER'S NOTE
Although the advice and information in this book are
believed to be accurate and true at the time of going to
press, neither the authors nor the publisher can accept any
legal responsibility or liability for any errors or omissions
that may have been made nor for any inaccuracies nor for
any loss, harm or injury that comes about from following
instructions or advice in this book.

CONTENTS

Introduction

For many people salt is just a white granular substance you sprinkle from a salt cellar on to your chips (French fries). Using salt to season food is a habit that many adults acquired as children, from parents. We just use it because it is there. How many people have you seen reach for the salt, even before tasting the food placed in front of them? It seems to me an assumption that the food won't be tasty unless smothered in sodium chloride. What about other flavours that are completely covered by the salt?

Salt is a commodity that we cannot do without. Every species of living creature needs the sodium in salt, but through changes during evolution, social groupings and civilization we now consume far more than we need. In fact, too much salt can cause as much or more harm than too little. I can't recall hearing of many people in my experience suffering salt deficiency, whereas I know plenty with high blood pressure.

The salt on the table is just the tip of the iceberg. It is everywhere in our daily lives.

Its industrial uses are phenomenal. In fact, only a small percentage of the salt produced in the world is used for food preservation or seasoning. It may yet contribute in some way to renewable energy sources.

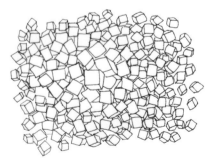

Historically, salt has been the cause of wars, uprisings and revolutions. It has been taxed all over the world, used as money and has been a powerful force in the economic rise and fall of civilizations. Religions, ceremonies and rituals rely on salt. You can't really ignore it.

This book explores many themes in a light-hearted fashion. While we can learn from history and we can take advice from scientists, now is, perhaps, the time to listen to advice and evidence from the medical world and not take their words with a pinch of salt!

What is Salt?

The term salt also specifically refers to sodium chloride, or common table salt, which is a crystalline compound. It has widespread uses as a food preservative and for seasoning. It is formed by the action of sodium on dry hydrogen gas and chlorine, which causes sodium chloride crystals to form. The chemical name for sodium chloride is NaCl. The 'Cl' part is easy to understand, but it doesn't really help explain why sodium is called Natron, so we'll go back a bit in terms of chemical understanding and historical evidence, to explain a little about sodium and natron; knowing a little about the properties of sodium helped me to understand why sodium chloride is such an important substance, and why, like so many other trails in this series on basic substances and their many benefits, we have a lot to thank the Ancient Egyptians for.

SODIUM

Sodium exists as more than a trace element in the stars and the sun and is the sixth most abundant element on the earth's crust, making up an estimated 2.8 per cent. Sodium, along with potassium, is classed as a soft metal but is not found naturally as a metal. It is found in a wide distribution as compounds with other substances, the most familiar being sodium chloride or table salt. Other salts of sodium are found in many rocks and in nearly all soil types. These include halides, silicates, carbonates, sulphates and nitrates. Sodium occurs throughout the rocky crust of the earth as feldspar, a silicate of sodium, and in various other rocks. Like potassium, sodium is a soft metal with a silvery white lustre. It tarnishes in the air and is one of the most reactive of metals.

Early civilizations knew about the benefits of sodium, although as potassium compounds were very similar in appearance, they thought they were the same substance. Records exist of saltpetre from potassium being used to make glazes for pots in Mesopotamia 17-centuries BC and the Egyptians used sodium carbonate 16 centuries BC for making glass. They also used natron for embalming and preserving.

The ancient Egyptians appreciated beauty so much they protected and preserved it even after death by mummification with natron, a white crystalline mixture of sodium bicarbonate, sodium carbonate, sodium chloride and sodium sulphate. It was mined from dry lake beds and from the banks of the River Nile. The area of Wadi-el-Natrun lies 23 m (25 yds) below sea level and gets its name from the natron. Known to be mildly antiseptic as well as a good exfoliant and drying substance, it was, all in all, a perfect base for adding oils and fragrances used to preserve the dead. The fragrances exemplified spirituality and beauty and served to cover up the foul odours of decaying flesh, which conjured up or summoned particular deities. So you not only had to look good but also smell divine, even in the intense heat of Egypt, without refrigeration or air conditioning!

Sodium chemicals today are used widely in synthetic chemistry as drying agents and reducing agents. Sodium has also been used in the manufacture of photoelectric cells. Its high heat capacity and conductivity make it useful as a heat transfer medium. It is lighter than water and can be cut with a knife at room temperature. It reacts with water to give hydrogen and sodium hydroxide, so it is an extremely active chemical which easily unites with oxygen. The metal is, therefore, usually kept immersed in an inert liquid for safety. It is used
in some nuclear reactors and sodium lights give that characteristic yellow illumination to many of our roads and towns. This works by gaseous sodium glowing in a tube which has voltage passed through it.

PROPERTIES OF SODIUM CHLORIDE

Sodium chloride forms symmetrical crystals. A salt in chemical terminology is produced by the reaction of an acid with a base. A salt is a positive ion of a base and the negative ion of an acid, producing a neutral product. The larger chloride ions form a cube arrangement while the gaps are filled with smaller sodium ions. Each ion is therefore surrounded by six ions of the other type.

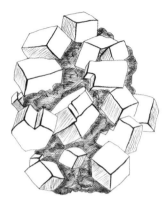

The same structure is found in many other minerals. The crystals are said to be isometric, meaning that they have three axes of symmetry, all equal in length and lying at 90 degrees from each other. The colour of the salt is dependent on its purity, but it is normally colourless to white. It may also be light blue, dark blue, yellow, orange, green, grey and pink. The colour is determined by bacterial debris trapped inside the lake or water source which evaporated. These coloured crystals are highly sought after by rock collectors.

THE SOLUTION
Salt's affinity for water means that it can be easily dissolved in a solution, as any upper Key Stage 2 Primary pupils will tell you. Evaporation of water content will return the salt to its previous solid condition. At 20°C (68°F) 100 g (4 fl oz) of water will dissolve 36 g (1½ oz) of salt. The higher the temperature of the water, the greater the amount of salt that will be dissolved.

SPECIFIC GRAVITY
The specific gravity of salt is 2.165, which means that salt is 2.165 times heavier than water at 0°C, 32°F.

MOHS SCALE OF HARDNESS
The Mohs scale of mineral hardness characterizes the scratch resistance of various minerals through the ability of a harder material to scratch a softer one. It was created in 1812 by the German mineralogust Friedrich Mohs and

is based on ten minerals that are readily available: Talc is 1, gypsum is 2, calcite has a hardness of 3 and diamond, the hardest mineral, 10. Halite has a hardness of 2.5, meaning that you can scratch it with a fingernail but not with a bronze coin.

MELTING POINT
Salt will melt at 427°C (800°F) and vaporize beyond this temperature. I haven't, obviously, put this to the test, being mainly concerned with Primary Science, but it might be of interest further up the scale of scientific enquiry!

BOILING POINT
Boiling point is 1,413°C. Again, I take this on trust, having neither the means, nor the inclination, to put it to the test.

ELECTROLYSIS OF SALT
Under an electrical current, molten salt decomposes to form metallic sodium and chlorine. When salts dissolve in water they are called electrolytes.

Salt is hygroscopic, which means that it will absorb water from damp atmospheres, above 75 per cent relative humidity. Below this, it will dry out.

SOURCES OF SODIUM CHLORIDE
There are three ways of extracting salt for processing:

- Rock salt, called halite
- Evaporated sea salt
- Natural brines

ROCK SALT

Halite, the mineral form of sodium chloride, occurs in rocks, commonly mudstones, but is present in a range of rocks from different geological eras, as masses and beds. The deposits are the residue of evaporated seas, lakes and salt flats. A bed of rock salt lying near the surface can be excavated like any other mineral. Some of the beds can be 350 m (383 yds) thick and lie under wide areas of landscape. High quality deposits need only to be ground and sieved for processing. Deposits with impurities may be melted and leached with dilute hydrochloric acid.

The salt is then washed, first with brine and then with fresh water, dried and ground to give crystals of the desired size. Deeper deposits can be extracted by pumping water down under pressure to dissolve the salt deposits before the brine is collected and treated.

Thirty per cent of the salt produced in the UK is from rock salt, produced mainly for de-icing roads. The rest is produced from brine, mostly by the chemical industries as a raw material. Some is evaporated to produce white salt. Britain has huge reserves of salt, mainly located in England, with some in Northern Ireland. Some of the largest halite deposits in Europe are to be found in the UK, Germany, France, Poland, Hungary, Romania and Austria. Other huge deposits are found in the USA and Canada, particularly the Appalachians, under New York, Ontario, the Michigan Basin, Utah, Ohio, Kansas, New Mexico and Nova Scotia. Pakistan, Iran, Russia and China also have important salt deposits. Another important halite deposit is to be found in salt domes.

SALT DOMES
Salt domes are formed when beds of rock containing quantities of evaporate minerals, such as halite, gypsum and anhydrite, are squeezed up through other rocks above. They intrude or push up vertically through the overlying, sedimentary rocks, creating pip-like masses of salt, or diapirs, because they are more buoyant, low density rock types. As they push up, they pierce the rocks above and create anticlines or upward folds in the surface of the earth. The mushroom-shaped domes produced make traps for hydrocarbons, such as natural gas, oil and coal. Salt domes are found along the coasts of Texas and Louisiana in the USA, Germany, Spain, the Netherlands, Romania and Iran. Naturally, the presence of a salt dome can arouse interest from oil and petroleum companies.

SALT GLACIERS

If these rising salt domes or diapirs breach the
surface of the earth they can produce salt glaciers,
as are found in the Zagros Mountains of Iran. The salt
may be mixed with clay and will move more during
the winter months when there is more moisture around,
than in the summer. Movement of salt will mean that
the flow spreads in tongue-like masses downward by
gravity into the surrounding area for many kilometres,
just like real glaciers.

SALT PANS

Salt pans are desert features, usually appearing as
a shiny white expanse of flat land covered in salt and
other minerals which have accumulated over thousands
of years. They signify where there was once water
which, unable to drain away, was evaporated faster than
any precipitation could collect. The crust of salt may
cover a muddy trap underneath, so should be treated
with care. They have provided ideal conditions for
aircraft runways and various land speed attempts,
as at the Bonneville Rock Desert in Nevada. Another
site in Nevada hosts an annual arts festival called the
Burning Man Festival. The largest salt pans in the world
is Salar de Uyuni, near Potosi in Bolivia. It covers
10,582 sq km (4,085 sq miles) and is 25 times bigger
than the Nevada flats.

Salt pans are found next to large areas of water, such as
coasts, lake shores or river deltas. They flood during
storms and mixtures of minerals result. The deposits can
appear zoned, like rings around a dirty bath. Sulphates
and carbonates collect around the edges, with sodium
chloride in the centre. Playa (Spanish for beach) or dry
lakebeds are the remains of the shore of a dried-up
endorheic lake. An endorheic lake is a closed basin,
where there is no water flowing in or out on the surface
as rivers or underground through rocks. This means that
the only water added to the lake is from rain or other
precipitation. The Dead Sea is an example of such a lake.
They can be found all over the world but are mostly
associated with deserts. The Black Sea was one such

lake until the Mediterranean Sea broke through the land separating the two. Such basins often have extensive salt pans although some are seasonal. Human activity in areas that were previously too dry for habitation means that many such lakes have been made smaller because of the building of dams. This may lead to higher salinity, concentrations of pollutants and disruption to ecosystems.

EVAPORATED SEA SALT

Sodium chloride is the chief chemical compound responsible for the saltiness of the sea. Four litres (1 gallon) of seawater contains between 1 per cent and 5 per cent solids, and sodium chloride is the most abundant of the salts in solution: over three-quarters of the solids are sodium chloride. Some seas are saltier than others. The polar seas have less salt content, whereas the Mediterranean and Red Seas, which are more enclosed, have much higher concentrations than open seas and oceans.

Specialized sea salts are produced in France, Ireland, Colombia, Sicily and the USA. These have different mineral contents and give a different flavour from table salt, which is pure sodium chloride. They are used in the cosmetics industry as well as in 'gourmet' cooking, although the actual salt content varies little from table salt.

Mineral	Average % of solids in sea water
Sodium chloride	77
Magnesium chloride	10
Magnesium sulphate	5
Calcium sulphate	3
Potassium chloride	3
Magnesium bromide	Trace
Calcium carbonate	Trace

NATURAL BRINES

Naturally occurring deposits of salt water are called brines and vast areas are found in the Dead Sea as well as parts of the USA (Death Valley), India, Australia and parts of Africa.

The Dead Sea covers an area of 1,049 sq km (405 sq miles). It is fairly free from sulphates and has a high percentage of potassium (38 per cent of solids), magnesium (53 per cent of solids) and bromine. Less than 8 per cent is sodium chloride. Weather conditions and temperatures mean that solar evaporation is possible for eight months of the year to process potassium and bromine as well as sodium chloride.

The brine from Kharaghoda in India is like sea water, but much more concentrated. In fact the brine is nearly saturated, meaning that the water has dissolved as much salt as possible. British brines contain chlorides of barium and strontium, not usually found in brines. These were found at great depths during test drilling for petroleum. Similar brines have been discovered in deep wells in locations in the USA.

EXTRACTION OF SODIUM CHLORIDE AND THE MANUFACTURE OF SALT

At one time nearly all the salt used commercially was produced from the evaporation of sea water. Today, 10 per cent of the world's salt requirements is produced by solar evaporation. It is the least complicated of mineral industries, needing only a source of salt water or rock salt and sunlight to evaporate the water content. Commercial production of salt comes from rock salt, sea water and natural brines. Artificial brines are created by pumping water into underground salt beds and a considerable amount of commercial salt is derived from this method.

SOLAR EVAPORATION

Solar evaporation is the oldest method of producing salt, having been used for thousands of years and probably originating along the shores of the Mediterranean and Red Seas. Its use is only practical in warmer climates where the evaporation rate exceeds the amount of rainfall by about 75 cm (30 in). This is called a negative evaporation rate. Basically the brine is allowed to evaporate to a specific gravity of about 1.21. This means that the brine is 1.2 times as dense as water. Impurities can be removed during this stage. The brine is then fed into three or four pans or shallow ponds for evaporation by the sun to start crystallization and where the concentration of salt gradually increases. In the final pan the specific gravity rises to 1.25 or 1.26. The salt crystals are washed with saturated brine and then fresh water.

The principle is the same, whether in the USA, West Indies, India or Africa. The salt, called bitterns, can then be used to make potash, bromine, magnesium chloride and magnesium sulphate (Epsom salts). The equipment might be more upmarket, but the method is the same.

In the Dead Sea area, dye is added to the water to allow more heat to be absorbed. Solar evaporation can take from one to five years to produce salt.

The solar evaporation ponds in San Francisco Bay produce about 700,000 tons per year. Commercial production began in 1854, although Native Americans had collected salt long before then. The brine is only 2.5 per cent sodium chloride compared with 3.5 per cent in sea water. Evaporation continues through a series of ponds until the brine is saturated and it is then fed into the crystallizer. The salt crystals collect in the bottom of the bed. The remaining dark red liquid brine, packed with magnesium and other minerals, is drained off to leave pure sodium chloride in a layer about 10–20 cm (5–8 in) thick. Huge machines like snowploughs scrape the salt up for processing. Salt harvesting in this way is seasonal, usually lasting from September until December, with a 24-hour operation in place to harvest before bad weather sets in.

This same cycle operates in the Camargue region in the south of France. The huge delta where the River Rhone meets the Mediterranean Sea is made up of inland salt lakes and marshes. Sea salt is the most important harvest of the region. Salt forms as the huge brine pans evaporate over the summer months and result in enormous mounds of salt crystals up to 8 m (26 ft) high, called camelles. During the summer up to 15,000 tons per day may be produced, when these salt plains look like a desert. Such salt marshes provide wonderful sites for wildlife, wildfowl and plant species adapted to salt water.

In the UK a very small amount of sea salt is produced by evaporation of sea water at Maldon in Essex.

METHODS USING OTHER FORMS OF HEAT

In areas where the salt can be mined by creating a solution of brine but solar evaporation is not viable, artificial heat is used to recover the salt. In days gone by salt was boiled to a concentrate over open fires. You can read about these methods in the chapter 'Salt Throughout History', but nowadays multiple-effect vacuum evaporators and open crystallizers are widely used.

GRAINER OR OPEN CRYSTALLIZATION METHOD

The first stage is to pump the brine, whether natural or man-made, into settling tanks, and calcium, sulphate and magnesium compounds are removed with chemical treatment using lime and sodium hydroxide. The brine is fed into a long open trough called a grainer which is heated by steam coils at a temperature slightly below that of the brine already in the grainer. The brine residue, or bitterns, is then removed on a regular basis, or continuously in very big operations. Evaporation happens at the surface of the solution and the crystals remain held there by surface tension, as they continue to grow at the top edges in what look like upside-down, hollow pyramids called hoppers. These eventually sink and stop growing, and when they are recovered they are like flakes. This type of salt is used by many consumers in the food industry.

MULTIPLE-EFFECT VACUUM EVAPORATORS

Most of the salt produced in colder climates comes from rock salt and most of this is produced by using multiple-effect vacuum evaporators. In these evaporators a series of chambers is used, each with a greater level of vacuum or 'effect'. The brine boils off through the action of the vacuum. This method is much more efficient and uses a lot less energy than open pans. It also produces very pure salt. Early evaporator vessels were made of cast iron, were not suitable for the pressures necessary and were limited to three effects. For the last half-century or so, steel has been used, allowing for up to six effects.

ALBERGER PROCESS

This is a combination of the grain and vacuum methods. It produces cubic crystals by the graining method and then uses a partial vacuum to create a cross between flakes and seed crystals. The salt is removed by centrifugal force and dried. The energy used for this method amounts to just over twice that for the vacuum method but only a quarter of that used by the open pan grainer method.

SALT IN THE UK

Salt can be extracted from great depths. Water is forced down a shaft which dissolves the salt. The brine is then pumped to the surface. Mined rock salt can also be extracted in huge lumps, which are crushed and brought to the surface for processing or transporting. The purity of rock salt, or halite, depends on the extent of the thickness of the mudstone it is found with. In the UK salty rocks do not occur on the surface because groundwater dissolves the salt. Sometimes it is easier to extract as brine by pumping. Where the brine or halite has been taken away, large underground cavities are left behind. These provide ideal conditions for storing gas and have, in the past, been used for storing oil.

The UK is a large producer, with 95 per cent coming from England and the rest from Northern Ireland. Of the UK output about 70 per cent is extracted as brine and the rest as halite. Salt is now only produced commercially in Cheshire and in the North York Moors National Park, where it is mined alongside potash. Rock salt is usually in greater demand during bad weather, when it is used for de-icing. About 2 million tons of halite are produced each year. Britain is self sufficient in salt, although some exporting and importing goes on. White salt production is about 1 million tons per year, and UK consumption is declining overall, from 7 million tons in 1980 to about 5.5 million tons in 2004.

MINING IN THE UK

Salt mining began at Winsford Minen in 1844, but the mine was closed between the 1890s and 1928. The salt is taken from galleries about 8 x 20 m (26 x 65 ft), with 20 m (65 ft) pillars being left behind. Drilling and blasting used to be the main methods for extraction, but now a continuous mining machine, introduced in 2002, is used as well. The rock is crushed underground and no waste is generated.

Solution mining recovers about a quarter of the salt reserve and is just as it sounds. Once the salt deposit is located, water is forced under pressure into a cavity which forms in the underground salt bed, as the salt dissolves. These cavities, designed to maintain the overlying rocks, can be 145 m (475 ft) across and up to 200 m (656 ft) high. The final size and shape of the cavity can be controlled by the positioning of water injection tubes and a compressed air blanket, which prevents dissolution upwards. The whole process is monitored by sonar. Mudstone falls to the base of the cavity and when these holes are no longer required they are left filled with brine.

All of this seems like very small fry, compared with the USA, where about 29 million tons of dry salt are produced each year. Unsurprisingly, the USA is the world's leading producer.

GRADES OF SALT

REFINED SALT
About 7 per cent of refined salt is used as a flavour enhancer and food additive. The rest is used in paper, textile, soap and detergent manufacture. During the drying process anti-caking agents are usually added. These absorb humidity and stop the crystals sticking together.

TABLE SALT
Table salt is 95 per cent sodium chloride and usually contains minute quantities of sugar, as well as an anti-caking agent. The sugar stops the salt turning yellow in sunlight and prevents loss of iodine, which has been added as a trace dietary supplement since 1924. Table salt is usually used for cooking or adding at the table. In 1911, magnesium carbonate was first added.

OTHER ADDITIVES
In some countries, where fluoride is not added to drinking water, brands of salt are available with added fluoride. Folic acid (Vitamin B) is also added to some brands, especially important for women in pregnancy.

COMMON SALT

This is a technical term for salt that is neither fine nor coarse. In days gone by, the texture, volume and moisture content of salt was determined by an experienced worker, simply by holding it in the hand. Nowadays, this is all controlled by machines.

FINE SALT

Fine salt is produced at higher temperatures and the crystals are smaller than common salt. This was used to make block salt in the past, by putting it into a mould for baking over flues in a hothouse.

COARSE OR FISHERY SALT

This is a washed grade used in the stock feed, hide curing, poultry feed and pet food industries, as well as for salting fish. It was often called 14-day salt, that being the time taken to evaporate the brine to form crystals. It requires slow simmering over a cool heat.

SUPERFINE SALT

This is a high quality salt used in bread, processed meats, biscuits, soap manufacture, and chemical applications.

LOW SODIUM SALT

Reduced-sodium alternatives contain less sodium than standard salt but taste similar. Sodium is the part of salt that can lead to high blood pressure, but salt substitutes are not suitable for some people. Low salts use potassium instead of purely sodium.

UNREFINED OR SEA SALT

This salt is sometimes called *fleur de sel* and has distinctive flavours, depending on the region it comes from. A lot of people prefer this for cooking or as a condiment, but others advocate the refined salt in case a deficiency of iodine occurs. It's all a matter of taste, really. See the chapter 'Salt: Kill or Cure?' for the effects of too much or too little salt in the diet. Sea salt is also used in cosmetics and as a hair product.

KOSHER SALT
Salt used to prepare Jewish food has larger flakes or crystals and a more open granular structure. Today kosher, or koshering, salt is commonly used in commercial kitchens as it does not contain additives. Because kosher salt grains are larger than ordinary table salt it does not dissolve readily. Salt remains on the surface of the meat longer, allowing fluids to leach out of the meat. This type of salt is not recommended for baking, where little liquid is used.

BLACK SALT
Black salt is an unrefined mineral salt that is really pinkish grey. It has a strong sulphuric flavour. Black salt is mined in India. It is used extensively in Indian cuisine and is considered a cooling spice in Hindu medicine, where it is used as a laxative and an aid to digestion. It is also believed to relieve intestinal gas and heartburn. It is sometimes used by people with high blood pressure or on low-salt diets because of its lower sodium content. Chemically, black salt is almost pure sodium chloride, with iron and trace minerals.

PRAGUE SALT
Road grit salt.

Salt
Throughout
History

For centuries salt has been used as a commodity as well as for flavouring and preserving food. It has been argued that the ability to preserve food has greatly contributed to the development of societies and civilizations as we know them today. As well as a saver of lives, salt had been used as a bartering tool, payment for work, a taxable item and has contributed to the cause of wars and economic embargoes.

Man cannot survive without salt but it was a long time before it was consumed directly as a mineral. We all need sodium and chlorine in our bodies, but before salt became a trading commodity early man got all the salt he needed through eating fish, shellfish and meat. It is believed that salt eating developed when humans started to keep animals and grow crops, that is, when they became farmers rather than hunter gatherers. Relying on hunting for meat wasn't exactly a sound choice unless you could outrun the local wildlife. So from about 10,000 BC the proportion of meat and fish in the diet declined. People had to find salt for their domesticated animals as well as themselves, especially if they moved away from the coast to areas where shellfish were not easily available.

First records of salt use date back to 4000 BC, unsurprisingly in Egypt. Clearly the presence of salt helped such civilizations, near desert climates and close to the sea, to develop. We know that the ancient Egyptians used salt and other sodium minerals to preserve food and embalm their dead. Egyptian art and hieroglyphs show salt-making taking place around 1450 BC. Salt was available as exposed rock outcrops in arid regions and as dried deposits on the shores of seas and salt lakes. By 2000 BC people elsewhere had discovered that salt preserved food and stopped it rotting. It was used to preserve meat, fish and vegetables. Salt also made a contribution to the development of society, when people began to come together to trade this valuable commodity and to share expertise. Practices such as salting olives added variation to the diet. Salt was expensive because of the hard work involved in extracting it, collecting it and carrying it across land and water.

PHOENICIAN TRADING

The Phoenicians were great traders and began harvesting salt from the sea and exporting it to other countries. They flooded the plains along coastal areas with sea water and left it to dry in the sun. After the water had evaporated the collected salt could be sold. Of course, this meant that the value of salt gradually decreased in real terms because there a constant supply available. Trading helped to spread techniques and ideas to other coastal areas, where people could also exploit their own salt.

TRAVEL

The availability of salt meant that food which was seasonal could be kept fresh for longer thanks to brine solution or a sprinkling of salt. This also meant that people could travel greater distances before their food supplies ran out or were spoiled by hot weather. People were no longer limited in their travel and trading by seasonal variations.

It wasn't only sea salt that changed the nature of trading and travelling, however. Salt had been mined since the Iron Age, although production was very small and local to the communities it supported. But warmer and dryer climates made evaporation of brines a much easier process than having to excavate rocks to reach small deposits. The European production of sea salt centred around the Mediterranean Sea, where the brine had a high salt content and the sun shone regularly. Even so, overall it wasn't a particularly easy process and was governed by the solar evaporation rates. Changes in sea level in the Mediterranean prevented some civilizations from obtaining consistent salt supplies. This in turn made people migrate and conquer or stay and take the consequences of being overrun by others. Salt remained essential but expensive because of transport costs up rivers, across seas and overland. It was in the interests of the traders to make sure that costs stayed high so that they could become very rich. It wasn't long before someone had the bright idea of taxing salt.

CHINESE SALT

In China around 2200 BC, the Emperor Hsia Yu levied one of the first known taxes in the world, on salt. As early as 2700 BC a work called *Peng Tzao Kan Mu* was known. It contained medical knowledge and observations on 40 kinds of salt. It explained a system for extraction very similar to the open pan system known today. Much later, during the Late T'ang Dynasty (AD 755–907) in China, tax and labour services were disrupted by a breakdown in authority and by huge movements of population. This was brought under control by a new government monopoly on salt. By 780 this salt monopoly was producing a large percentage of the state's revenue. The state salt commission gradually took over the financial administration of southern and central China. Salt rules!

ROMAN TIMES

The Romans valued salt so highly that they controlled the price of it. They increased the cost to raise money for wars against their less civilized or less well organized neighbours, in order to expand their empire. They also lowered it to make sure that poorer citizens could afford to buy it. Maybe that's why Roman soldiers were paid at certain times with salt. That's where we get the word 'salary' from – see The Language of Salt, pages 152–3, for more details. *Salarium Argentum* was the name for the salt rations given to soldiers. This was a pretty shrewd move really, considering that the soldiers were expected to walk for days on end, often in unpleasantly hot conditions, and arrive fit and healthy, ready for a good fight! The salt would have been essential for their continued health.

The Romans were great engineers and road builders. This meant that the soldiers could march quickly and directly and also that salt could be easily moved around as Rome developed. The Via Salaria was a road that led from Rome to the Adriatic Sea where the shallow depth of water meant that there was a high salt content. Evaporation produced much more salt than the Tyrrhenian Sea, which was much closer to Rome.

At the beginning of the Roman period the sea level was a good 2 m (6 ft) below the present level. Salt-making was well established on the coasts of western Europe and the Mediterranean, until the vast, flat coastal areas ideal for making salt were gradually submerged. By about AD 400 the traditional Roman salt flats of Ostia and Aquilea had been irreparably flooded. Osia was the port of Rome and was moved inland three times. Rome needed to find more supplies of salt, or lose its empire.

WHAT'S IT WORTH?

In ancient Greece slave traders often bartered salt for slaves. A slave who failed to come up to the expectations of his master was said to be 'not worth his salt'.

In Tibet, the explorer Marco Polo wrote about salt as if it was as precious as gold, which it probably was. Gold was formed into thin rods and cut to certain lengths as currency. He noted that for smaller amounts of currency, cakes of salt were produced from brine springs by boiling to evaporate the water. After about an hour the salt could be pressed with symbols of the Grand Khan, dried and used as coins. Only officers of the Grand Khan could make this money. The salt coins appear to have increased in value the further they were carried from the towns into remote areas. This is not the only use of salt for actual money. Salt is still used as currency among the nomads of the Danakil Plains in Ethiopia.

POWER IN TIMBUKTU

By the 8th century Islam was spreading to West Africa and had travelled to Ghana and its empire. Mediterranean countries badly wanted gold but all they had to offer was a load of salt. In contrast, West African countries had plenty of gold but needed salt to survive. The Mali Empire was founded and trade in gold and salt prospered. In the Mali Empire the city of Timbuktu was the gateway to the Sahara and a prestigious seat of learning and civilization. It developed as a huge salt market, giving it power and wealth previously unimagined. Supplies of salt in an arid region provided the power to control life and death.

Between the 8th and 16th centuries trade between countries around the Mediterranean and West Africa thrived. The Sahara Desert stood in the path of the lucrative trade which was conducted by caravans of camels. The animals would be fattened up before setting off in their thousands. Guided by Berber tribesmen, safe passage was ensured. Runners were sent ahead to oases, to carry back essential supplies of water, enabling the huge distances to be covered safely. The camels could last weeks without food or water, but people could not. The merchants of the 12th century valued salt so highly that they reportedly paid for it by its weight in gold. Legends abounded that Timbuktu was very rich indeed and news of its wealth fuelled stories in Europe from countries who were importing the mineral. There are reports of up to 12,000 camels trekking 644 km (400 miles) across the Sahara Desert with cargoes of salt, some of which was exchanged for another valuable asset in the form of slaves.

THE SILENT TREATMENT
When language was a barrier to trade, silent trade or dumb barter was used, similar to methods known in the silk trade.

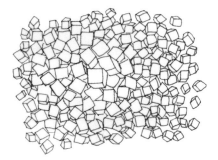

When merchants reached a settlement or trade area they beat great drums to summon the natives, who would not appear in the presence of the strangers. An alternative method was for the locals to beat a drum, light a fire or use some other form of signalling to attract the merchants. The merchants arranged their salt in piles, signalled and then withdrew. The local people then appeared and examined the goods, left a heap of gold beside each pile and retired. If the merchants were satisfied, they took the gold, beating their drums to signal completion of the deal. If the local people did not agree to the barter, they, in theory at least, had the option of removing some of their gold. I can't help wondering how much gold was traded for a lump of life-giving salt.

According to one Moorish proverb, 'The price of a negro is salt'.

ANCIENT SALT WORKS
Archaeologists know that there were many early attempts to quarry and mine salt. Salt tunnels containing stone hammers and axes have been found at numerous sites in Asia Minor, Armenia, South and North America. The Hallstadt salt mines in the Austrian Alps and the Italian mines were important in supporting prehistoric communities. Similar tools were used across all continents.

The earliest coastal salt manufacture depended on wide, flat coastal areas and in making use of natural depressions or lagoons. Later, man-made salt works were formed, called salterns. These were 15—20 cm (6—9 in) deep and had to be created at mid-tide level so that they would fill from the sea.

The Chinese developed the idea of drilling into a salt deposit with at least two holes. One was used to flood fresh water into the salt deposit while the second hole allowed the water to well up after dissolving the salt. They used bamboo pipes to reach brine at depths of up to 1,000 m (3,281 ft). This was then collected in the evaporation pans, where it could be concentrated again.

Very old solar pans are still in operation in the salt water swamps that lie in the bend of the Yellow River. Similar operations provided salt in Iran.

SALT ROUTES

During the later years of the Roman Empire and into the Middle Ages, salt continued to play a big part in economic development. Salt routes, such as the Old Salt Route in northern Germany, allowed towns like Lübeck and the trading company the Hanseatic League to be powerful forces in the Middle Ages. Salt was mined near Luneburg, associated with salt for 1,000 years, and called 'white gold'. From Luneburg, known as the City of Salt, the salt route led to Lübeck from where cartloads of salt were sent by ship to various places around the Baltic. At its destination it was used to preserve fish caught by fishing boats across the Baltic Sea. The fish were then exported to other parts of Europe. After 1398 the salt could be transported by water along the Stecknitz Canal, one of the oldest canals in Europe. The journey didn't get any shorter, however, lasting about 20 days, either by canal or cart.

NO EASY SOLUTION

For evaporation methods to work properly it would take an estimated 50,000 cubic metres of sea water spread over 100,000 square miles of solar evaporation area. All this would produce only 1,000 tons of salt a year. Not such an easy proposition! You also needed a hot sun with a warm breeze and a steady sea level. This made the Mediterranean, where the tide fluctuates by only a few centimetres, ideal, whereas other major seas and oceans have tides of several metres. When the sea was a metre or two below its present level there were plenty of areas to choose from, but as climates changed and sea levels rose, the right land became less easy to find.

Deltas of rivers like the Nile, Rhône and the Euphrates also changed and the establishment of new ponds became more difficult. Brine production from one level of concentration to the next could take months or even years. A change in climate conditions, or even a minor fluctuation in ocean levels, could have a serious effect on coastal salt-making. Mining salt from the ground or collecting from inland salt springs or brine lakes like the Dead Sea became the only alternative in some areas. Evidence still exists along the shores of the Dead Sea, where you can find solar pans that were used by ancient salt-makers.

SOUTH AMERICA

Before the 1500s the main applications of salt in Mexico and South America related to rituals, staying alive and preserving fish. The Mayans enjoyed a good living until the Spanish conquest, when the Spanish took over numerous salt sources. Before long they had taken control of a major part of the continent. A process developed in Mexico whereby silver was leached from ore with a sodium solution. This process became a major industry, and the demand for salt increased. The vast Yucatan resources of evaporated salt met most of the needs.

SALT IN THE UK

EARLY SALT WORKS IN BRITAIN

About 250 million years ago salt was laid down in what is now Britain, but what was, at the time, a shallow inland sea close to the equator. Continental drift accounted for the migration of land masses northwards. Some of the former inland seas, now salt beds, were left exposed and dissolved away but others lay buried as rock salts, waiting to be discovered. Britain has few sites where rock salt can be extracted but in Cheshire the deposits are fairly close to the surface at about 50 m (150 ft). This didn't stop people 2,000 years ago from discovering that the water draining into the ground dissolved the rock salt into brine and created salty springs. What could be more convenient for the exploitation of the salt?

IRON AGE SALT

The earliest examples of salt works date back to prehistoric times. Archaeologists have found the remains of rough pottery and supporting pillars, known as briquetage, which were used for salt-making. These Iron Age remains have been found along the east coast, in East Anglia and Essex, as well as Lincolnshire. Clay pans were used which were 60 cm (24 in) wide, 120 cm (48 in) long and 12 mm (½ in) thick. These were supported on pillars and brine was evaporated in smaller vessels which were broken to get out the lump of salt produced. In Cheshire, Wales and western England the finished salt was sold or given out in the vessels it was made in.

SALTERNS

The word 'saltern' on a map denotes the existence of medieval salt works. A saltern was often a clay hut used for salt production and could be set up wherever conditions were favourable, but was more commonly found in conjunction with other industries or with farming. Salterns were often to be found near tanning works in areas of pastoral farming. This meant that there was a supply of salt for curing hides and skins close to the supply of animals. Salterns also needed to be near a market, where the salt could be sold.

Then all you needed was a gently sloping coastline, a tidal river or a salt marsh, and a reliable fuel for evaporating the salt.

The huts had a hole in the roof to allow smoke to escape. Large fires were lit beneath clay troughs of brine, rather than sea water, to evaporate water, leaving salt crystals. The brine was produced by passing fresh water over salt-rich sand or mud collected from beneath the sea and packed into clay troughs.

IT'LL ALL COME OUT IN THE WASH

During both Roman and medieval times the area around the Wash in eastern England fitted the bill perfectly. The tide brought in the salt water, the saltings gave plenty of pasture areas for animal grazing and the Fens provided peat for fuel. The brine was evaporated by the sun into a slurry-like mess of salt, sand and silt. This was then cleaned with sea water so that the sand and silt settled. The brine was then taken off the top and poured into shallow pans made from the local clay. These were set on clay pillars over peat fires to finish the evaporation process. Dried salt could then be removed and sold.

Other salterns existed wherever the land was low enough and the conditions were right. Some certainly existed in the south on the Pevensey Levels in Sussex, close to the now inland site of Pevensey Castle, originally built by the Romans on the coast, and at the Great Salterns near Southsea, where the inlet of Langthwaite Harbour provided the right conditions. Much of the salt collected here went straight to Portsmouth for naval use.

SUPPLY AND DEMAND

Both Roman and medieval salt pans have been discovered in Cheshire. These were made of lead and were about 1 metre square (1 square yard) in area. The names of some of the Roman salt makers are written on the lead pans, so we know that Viventius and Veluvius worked there. Middlewich was called Salinae at the time, demonstrating salt's importance even back then. British salt making was already established along the coasts, but the Roman conquest brought new needs and demands.

The nearly saturated brine at inland spring sites needed much less fuel to evaporate the liquid than the weaker sea water. By AD 60, military camps were established at Chester and Middlewich. The Chester site acted as a supply port and control station for Wales's lead and silver mines and Middlewich commanded the River Dane. Here, the Romans created their own salt works.

DOMESDAY
Salt-making continued after the Roman occupation through to Anglo Saxon times and later attracted the attention of the Vikings, although there were few changes in methods of production except that the lead pans increased in size after the Norman conquest. Salt works are mentioned in the Domesday Book of 1086, which also included information on which manors owned coastal salt works. The number was considerable and these were mainly concentrated along the east and south coasts, where solar evaporation was harnessed on a seasonal basis. This meant that less fuel was needed for final evaporation. Before 1066, Droitwich in Worcestershire seems to have been much more important than other inland sites and produced more than the whole of Cheshire. A total of 318 salt houses were recorded in the Domesday Book.

Lead remained in use until the end of medieval times, when iron pans were found to be more effective, and when coal replaced wood as a fuel for heating brine. With this new, better fuel the size of the pans increased steadily until they reached about 6 x 9 m (20 x 30 ft). This meant that production could be stepped up considerably. Pan houses have been excavated at Nantwich in Cheshire and Droitwich.

PRESERVATION
Up until the Industrial Revolution the main use for salt was the preservation of food, so obviously as the population of Britain grew the demand for salt increased as well. Between 1066 and the Black Death in the mid-14th century the population doubled. Coastal salt works traded with the continent and salt was also imported from the Bay of Biscay area, along with wine from

Gascony. Henry II married Eleanor of Aquitaine in 1152 and much of south-west France belonged to the English crown. Trade was prosperous and the salt merchants formed a Fraternity of Salters.

PLAGUE

With the Black Death the demand for salt dwindled, along with the population, which was reduced by a half. Coupled with rising sea levels this virtually saw off the exports from Fenland ports and instead coastal salt-makers started to import grey Bay salt to refine. This grey salt was re-crystallized from sea water to give white salt for home consumption as well as for re-exporting for a profit.

In Cheshire the plague meant there was a drop in demand as well. Middlewich and Northwich belonged to the crown and taxes were levied on making, selling and buying fuel for processing. In Nantwich, where ownership remained with the gentry or with monasteries, the pattern was different. By the mid-14th century salt houses had spread to both sides of the river and 'walling land' was designated to prevent further expansion. By the mid-1600s there were 216 lands of ancient inheritance, each with six lead pans. Strict rules governed shares of the brine pit and a rota was set up stating the days when each owner could access the brine. This was called 'walling the kale'.

RECOVERY

By Tudor times the population had recovered to the level before the Black Death. Supplies still came from coastal areas and from France, but now also from Scotland. By now, coal was available as fuel and iron pans had replaced the lead ones, thankfully. I can't help wondering how many people died of lead poisoning during the previous centuries of salt production. Queen Elizabeth I gave a patent to Tyneside producers to try to make Britain self-sufficient in salt, but this proved unsuccessful.

WHERE'S MY PAN GONE?

The use of coal instead of wood as fuel forced a change from lead to iron pans, as the coal actually melted the lead pans. The aim with coal was to boil and evaporate quickly, which didn't fit well with the Nantwich walling rules of having your days for working fixed, making it essential to keep the fires stoked and burning intensively. In the early 17th century a method of distributing the brine in overhead wooden channels was developed and the flow was measured. A common cistern was installed and the fires under the pans were only allowed to burn for set times. Ingenious! Gradually lead pans were replaced with iron ones, although, of course, iron rusts and corrodes through constant contact with salt and water. The rust also stained the salt. Lead was much easier to work and recycle, although, obviously, with the benefit of hindsight, not a healthier option. Nantwich was slower to change than other salt works, and the standard-sized six lead pans were each replaced with four iron ones by 1650.

SALT ROCKS

In 1670 deep rock salt reserves were discovered in Cheshire. This led to some drilling for commercial exploitation through brine production, either by dissolving the rock salt or by developing the existing brine springs. Some of the mined salt was used to strengthen the content of weaker brines. Shallow mines flooded as a result and pumping of the brine water caused the roof pillars to collapse. Many of these now form lakes throughout the area. This led to damaging subsidence on the surface, often at some distance from the point of extraction, surprising many people at the time. This subsidence finally stopped modern extraction in Worcestershire in 1971 and Staffordshire in 1970. Lancashire ceased to produce brine in 1993.

Eventually smaller salt works couldn't keep up with the cheaper production costs at the Cheshire sites and larger producers took over. Conditions in the salt works were appalling, with whole families employed to look after the pans in hot, steamy and smoky conditions. Sixteen-hour shifts were not unheard of.

A LION AMONG SALT WORKS

The Thompson family, long associated with the salt industry from the 18th century, created a vast range of industries associated with the mining of rock salt, including evaporating brine, running a brick works and a boatyard. They also had interests in a colliery and imported timber, making raw materials for mining easily available. The Lion Salt Works at Northwich continued to expand and adapt to market changes.

By 1900, fuel and labour costs were reduced by the introduction of the vacuum evaporation system. This didn't make the required grade of salt that the old, open pan methods had provided, but gradually the cheaper salt vacuum crystals were accepted. People became ever more concerned about the subsidence caused and by the poor air quality around the old open pan salt works. The Lion Works continued to operate until, in 1960, it was the only open pan salt works in operation. It closed in 1986, when Nigeria, a major purchaser of the salt produced, was engaged in civil war, resulting in a collapse of the market. A museum now re-enacts the methods used at Northwich.

LOCAL SALT FOR LOCAL PEOPLE

At first the salt produced from Cheshire brine was only for local use and had little impact on London markets. The main form of transport was packhorse and trails spread from the salt towns to the surrounding area. After the industrial revolution, when coal was available, river transport increased and the construction of canals expanded. The Weaver Navigation was completed in 1710 and the Trent and Mersey Canal opened in 1777. The railway system started to develop and Cheshire had a big advantage over the small brine producers along the coast.

TECHNOLOGICAL IMPROVEMENTS

During the 18th century pumping technology improved and allowed for deeper brine shafts. Horse gins or water wheels were used to raise the brine. The first steam engine to drive a brine pump was used in 1777 and was based on Watt's 1775 model. Edward Salmon's new Lawton Salt Works used the new canal network to reach Liverpool and eastwards to the Potteries. By 1790 the canal network had expanded and Lawton salt could be shipped to Hull. Lawton Salt Works was the first company to use hessian bags for salt instead of the traditional wicker baskets.

As a result of improvements in the salt-based chemical industry, changes were afoot elsewhere. The major uses of salt had been the preservation of food and flavouring, although the meat aspect had widened to include leather curing and tanning. Salt was also used to embalm the dead. In the 1770s salt was first used with sulphuric acid to make hydrochloric acid for bleaching. The textile and soap industries had previously been dependent on importing alkali in the form of potash, but in the 1760s salt was used as a raw material for making alkali. The invention of the Leblanc process in 1783 provided a cheaper alternative. You can read more about this in the section on industrial uses. Production also needed sulphur, coal and limestone, all available on Tyneside and in Glasgow. By the close of the 18th century salt was well and truly established as an industrial chemical and salt tax was abolished in order to promote this industry. This coincided with the end of the Napoleonic wars and renewed prosperity in Britain.

19TH CENTURY DEVELOPMENTS

During Victorian times salt was important for the development of the chemical industries. It became easier to mine salt in the second half of the 19th century, so it was more easily available in large quantities for industrial use and didn't rely on evaporating sea water or extraction of brine alone. Salt also became much cheaper. It has been suggested that the port of Liverpool expanded in the 1800s as a result of the salt dug from the Cheshire mines, which became a major world supplier during the 19th century. Liverpool certainly exported vast quantities of salt as well as coal and manufactured goods at this time.

After the repeal of salt tax in 1824, Merseyside grew as an alkali-producing area due to its proximity to the Cheshire salt deposits. Salt could be transported via the Weaver Navigation and the demand for salt from the home market and for export led to the development of a huge site at Winsford and another along the Trent and Mersey Canal. Salt works grew up elsewhere and soon there was a problem of overcapacity. This led to a merger in 1888 to form the Salt Union and standardized method and measures.

QUALITY AND GRADES

For many years the Cheshire salt had been considered unsuitable by the fishing industry as it was too fine. The coarser sea salt (Bay salt) was preferred for salting fish and continued to be imported from France, even when Britain was at war with the French in the 1740s. In 1748 Thomas Lowndes advocated an open pan method, involving slow evaporation in larger pans, which became the standard method. Alum was also added to produce clear, harder crystals. This produced the pyramidal hopper crystals seen in coarser salts and didn't need to be dried in a hothouse.

Other additives were also tried in addition to alum, egg white, blood and ale, including glue and soft soap. The glue increased the surface tension and the soap decreased it. Crystal size obviously affected density of the product. Where the product was sold by volume rather than weight, size of crystal could be a critical factor in profit margins.

Different markets required a range of crystal size, for example butter- and cheese-makers needed finer salt. Too much glue could make for a continuous crust of salt, which wasn't always desirable.

Pans were 7–7.5 m (24–25 ft) wide to allow for 3.5 m (12 ft) long rakes to draw salt from the centre of the pans. For fine pans, the length was about 12 m (40 ft). Fast fires heated and boiled the brine while also heating hothouses where the salt was dried over the course of about two weeks, before being crushed and processed into fine crystalline salt for dairy use. Common pans were about twice the length of fine pans and were kept at simmering temperature to produce large crystals. Salt for alkali-making formed after a day or two, but salt crystals for fisheries or tanneries might take two or three weeks to form. Drained salt was then transported directly, without drying.

20TH-CENTURY PRODUCTION

Vacuum evaporation, as described in the previous chapter, was a process developed from sugar refining. It was first applied to salt in the USA in the 1880s but the first commercial use for salt production in the UK was in 1901 in Middlewich. The Winsford Vacuum Plant of 1905 quickly followed and a much larger model was built six years later alongside the Manchester Ship Canal, at Runcorn. Vacuum works didn't replace open pans until later, but by the end of the 1930s it was apparent that they were taking over. Also, by this time, refrigeration was taking over many of the food preserving functions that salt had provided. In 1937 the Salt Union was taken over by ICI and cleaner, more efficient vacuum evaporators were developed. The Winsford open pans were closed down in the 1950s and all open pans in Middlewich had closed by 1970, leaving only the Lion Salt Works, providing specialized products for Nigeria until 1986. British Salt was formed in 1969.

Like most industries, the open pan method had its share of specialist vocabulary and unusual terms.

From Anglo Saxon times to around 1890 cone-shaped baskets called *barrows* were woven from hazel, in which the salt was placed. From the turn of the century *peg top* tubs were made by coopers, or barrel-makers, from elm wood. Later models called tubs were made in tapered wooden moulds of varying size.

A popular size was 80s, which weighed between 11 and 12 kg (28 lb). Workers had to *lump* the salt into the moulds. Their job, therefore, was known as *lumping*. These lumps had to be crushed before the salt could be used, but were often transported as lumps. *Lumpmen* stood on woven hurdles which created walkways between the ancient salt pans. The salt was put on hurdles in a wall of salt. *Wallers*, often women, raked the salt.

During the 16th century protein, in the form of blood, egg white or ale, was added to the brine to form a froth in which to trap suspended solids. This was called *froth flotation* and is still used in some mineral processing.

SALT DOME

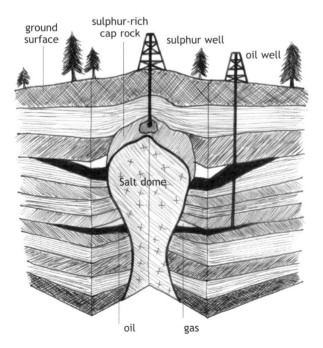

SALT TAXES

Salt has probably been one of the most taxed commodities of all times. From early times people have appreciated the need for salt and have cashed in accordingly.

ENGLISH SALT TAX

The Stuarts raised tax on salt, wine and tobacco in 1644 but after the Restoration Charles II sensibly chose not to tax salt. In 1693 William III reintroduced a salt tax, but luckily for the English poor, the tax was levied on the manufacturers instead of the consumers. Perhaps the French monarchy should have followed suit, thereby possibly avoiding losing both their throne and their heads. George III used salt tax in 1767 to pay for the American War of Independence.

The salt tax was collected by a whole host of officials and supervisors, weighers, watchmen and salt officers, who, despite their numbers, failed miserably to stop smuggling. Originally there were two collection groups, a Board of Customs for foreign trade and a Board of Excise for home trade. Home-produced salt was taxed at several times its market value and tax on imported salt was twice as much. There were cheaper rates for fishery salt, however, and for rock salt. The relatively heavy taxation on salt made it a favourite cargo for smuggling from Ireland to Wales at the end of the 17th century, and there seems to have been little enthusiasm on the part of the collectors to enforce the law. It is doubtful that the expense of collecting the tax justified the revenue it raised.

Exports of rock salt to Ireland were free of duty during most of the following century and so Ireland developed quite a large salt-refining industry along the coast. Imports lasted until the Cheshire rock salt industry took off. Another spin-off was that salt production along the west coast declined because the smuggling of refined salt back into England and Wales made salt-making unprofitable.

Meanwhile, in Ireland salt refining developed into a major industry, with exports to Russia, Scandinavia and America. The untaxed white salt helped to develop the butter industry until Ireland became a world leader in butter exports. The salt was also used for preserving fish, beef and pork. The fish came from Scotland and Sweden for processing before being barrelled and sent to the West Indies.

SALT TAXES IN FRANCE

Charles of Anjou levied a salt tax in 1259 to help pay for a war on the Kingdom of Naples. The *Gabelle*, or salt tax, was introduced across France in 1286 by Philip IV as a temporary source of revenue and was not finally seen off until the French Revolution in 1790, when it had become one of the most hated taxes in the country.

France had always produced salt along the Mediterranean and Atlantic coasts but was not one of the major trading nations, so salt became an important commodity. The government controlled a state monopoly and then made everyone over the age of eight buy a weekly minimum amount of salt at a fixed price.

The price varied in different parts of France, and six distinct regions each had their own salt granaries, dating from 1342. All producers were obliged to take their salt to the *greniers a sel* or risk having their entire supply confiscated. Of course, the *greniers* then sold the salt at a much higher price.

As you can imagine, a lot of smuggling and tax evasion took place. A fairly sophisticated method of buying salt in a region where the price was cheaper and selling it 'under the counter' at a higher price, but still cheaper than the official price, was rife. Smugglers like these risked being sent to the galleys if caught unarmed, or sentenced to death if found armed. Imagine having a large family and being forced to buy salt per head on a regular basis. Obviously nobody knew that too much salt is bad for you, especially for children!

From 1630 to 1710 the tax had increased tenfold. In 1675 a group in Brittany, known as the red bonnets, rebelled against the *Gabelle* and wrote down their grievances in the Peasant Code. As conditions went from bad to worse over the following decades and a series of bad harvests led to crop failure, the price of bread rose as well. Bread was the staple diet of the poorest peasants and starvation increased. By 1789 the price of bread had rocketed. The salt tax was hated by all and the towns and cities were full of hungry, angry peasants. The bread riots that followed turned into a main cause of the French Revolution.

While average taxes were higher in Britain, it was the poorer people in France who suffered more than the rich. The collection of the *Gabelle* was contracted out to a few chosen people who were allowed to charge even more for the salt than the government requested, allowing unequal tariffs to exist. When Louis XVI was deposed by the mob, the tax was repealed. Interestingly enough, it was re-introduced early in the 19th century and stayed until after the end of World War II, in 1946.

SALT AND INDEPENDENCE IN INDIA

A high salt tax imposed by the British in India provoked a 322 km (200-mile) march led by Mahatma Gandhi in 1930. Gandhi decided to make the tax on salt high profile in a non-violent protest.

Although salt was acknowledged as a basic necessity, it had been taxed in India even before the era of British rule, although not to the same extent. The local rulers had a variable tax imposed, dependent on the religion of the traders. Those who were Muslim paid 2.5 per cent, whereas Hindus were charged 5 per cent. The traders were taxed as they travelled up the River Ganges.

Tax increased under the umbrella of the East India Company, who had a monopoly and doubled the price of salt. This only encouraged illegal trading, so an inland customs line was set up between the 1840s and 1880s, stretching 3,701 km (2,300 miles). This line was guarded and patrolled by a staggering 12,000 men. The barrier was really a hedge of thorny trees and bushes with walls and ditches. It was almost impossible to cross without being stopped or incurring injuries. It has been suggested that many thousands of Indian subjects suffered salt deprivation as a result. Even after the Great Hedge was dismantled and forgotten, the tax remained.

Gandhi used the salt tax as an expression of disapproval of British colonial rule. The monopoly on salt continued and it was stated that the sale or production of salt by anyone other than the British was a punishable offence. Although salt was readily available along the coast, locals were not allowed to collect it for themselves, but had instead to buy it from the government. Gandhi devised a means of protest that brought together people across class, religion and regions, as the tax impacted on the whole of India, and he created a popular following.

Gandhi first wrote to the Viceroy, Lord Irwin, informing him that he was about to disregard the salt laws. This was reported in newspapers and when Irwin failed to reply Gandhi and about 80 followers set off from Sabarmati Ashram on 12 March, 1930 for the coastal village of Dandi, over 322 km (200 miles) away. Thousands joined him along the wayside and the British were powerless to stop the protest because Gandhi had not asked anyone to join him. The event was covered by the press and on arrival in Dandi on 5 April, Gandhi was interviewed and able to make a powerful statement before collecting some muddy salt which he boiled in sea water to produce salt, saying 'With this, I am shaking the foundations of the British Empire'. He encouraged others to copy him, wherever and whenever they wished, rather than purchasing salt from the British.

This symbolic gesture started a non-violent programme of civil disobedience which spread across the country. Along with a boycott on British-made goods, salt was made and sold illegally along the coastal areas and the British government had locked up over 60 000 people by the end of the month. Gandhi was arrested under a law passed in 1827, but the world had heard about the protest. After his release he continued to work for Indian independence, which was finally achieved in August 1947.

SALT TAX IN ITALY

Until 1975, salt tax was collected through monopolies and the imposition of import customs. The state had a monopoly on the manufacture and sale of salt, and fixed the final market price, which included the tax rate of about 70 per cent. Discount prices were fixed on salt for agricultural and industrial uses and production was tax-free in Sicily, Sardinia and in a few towns.

A BRIEF SUMMARY OF SALT HISTORY IN THE USA

The first Europeans to reach America noted native groups harvesting salt from the sea and it is thought that they had been producing salt for at least 500 years before that. The Hopi people in the south-west had ceremonial salt mines. The USA has massive reserves of salt available, although there have been times in its history when a shortage of salt caused major upheaval.

During the 15th century Portuguese and Spanish fleets used a method of salting fish on board ship, whereas the French and British fleets took their catch ashore to dry and salt on racks. This is how Britain and France became the first white settlers in Newfoundland since the Vikings.

SOME DITCH!
The Erie Canal, connecting the Great Lakes to New York's Hudson River in 1825, was hailed as an engineering marvel, although nicknamed 'the ditch that salt built'. Salt tax revenues paid for half the cost of construction of the canal and salt was the main cargo to use the waterway.

STRATEGY WHICH DIDN'T WORK
Part of the British strategy during the American War of Independence (1763–89) was to deny salt to the rebels, so Americans had to learn to make their own salt. The Iroquois had a treaty with the State of New York to provide salt reservations. Reports from 1654 show that Onondaga Indians were making salt by boiling brine from springs, as were the native people of West Virginia in

1755. Larger-scale production was under way by 1800 and drilling for concentrated brine soon followed.
Solar salt works survived without the ideal climate for evaporation by means of movable sheds over evaporating pans. Sites on San Francisco Bay, California in 1770 and later at Great Salt Lake in Utah, in 1847, were important to the economy.

AMERICAN CIVIL WAR
Full-scale production from open pits began in 1862, during the Civil War, and underground mining started in 1869. Confederate salt production facilities in Saltville, Virginia and Louisiana, were early targets of the Union Army. In 1864 the North fought for 36 hours to capture Saltville, where the salt works were considered crucial to the Rebel army. This was the last important salt processing works in the hands of the Confederates and essential to the army. Confederate President Jefferson Davis was so concerned about salt supplies that he offered to waive military service in return for tending coastal salt kettles to supply the South's war effort. The salt was needed to tan leather, dye cloth for uniforms and to preserve meat. The lack of salt was lowering morale considerably among the population as well.

SALT IN RUSSIA

Salt production has influenced all spheres of life in Russia and is the oldest branch of Russian industry. The struggle for supremacy over salt resources led to bloody wars and to uprisings like the 1648 Moscow salt riot, when the masses revolted against overburdening salt taxes.

At the end of the 16th century many salteries owned by associations of townspeople, peasants or by monasteries, were taken over by force. Monasteries, granted exemption from tax by the Tsar, made a good business out of salt, which was expensive to buy. The technology was quite sophisticated, with wells being drilled to a depth of 180 m (590 ft). Another means of making salt was to dig a canal from an existing lake to an artificial lake for extraction. Brine was then transported by pipe to salt works in the towns.

SALT STROGANOV

In the mid-16th century, Ivan the Terrible granted the Stroganovs, who were merchants, a charter that entitled them to a vast, uninhabited area extending 250 km (155 miles) along the banks of the River Kama. Mass settlement followed and they became the 'salt kings of Russia' owning, by the end of the 17th century, 233 salteries along the Kama around Perm. Until the middle of the 17th century, the main area of salt production in Russia was the northern region of Belomorye, but it was superseded by the Perm region as the main supplier of salt to the Russian State.

The name of Solikamsk means Salts of Kama and is well known throughout Russia as the 'salt cellar of Russia'. The industry was at its peak in the 17th century. After the state ownership was declared there was a decline until the 1870s. However, in 1887, the Ustj-Borovskoy salt factory was built and Solikamsk once again became the main salt producer of Russia.

SIBERIAN SALT MINES

Little information seems to be available about the Siberian salt mines, although they are referred to frequently because of the extremely harsh conditions and forced labour. The building of the Trans-Siberian Railway, completed in 1914, opened up the area for exploitation of massive mineral reserves, but before it was built convicts had to walk for three months to cover the 1,609 km (1,000 miles) over the Ural Mountains to the salt mines and labour camps around Irkutsk. By 1900, over one million people had been exiled and had made the long journey to the so-called salt mines, where they were in fact often mining gold, silver and copper, rather than salt. After the discovery of the mineral deposits within Siberia the use of exiled 'criminals' was the obvious answer.

The Industrial
Uses of Salt

A BRIEF SUMMARY OF THE EARLY HISTORY OF CHEMICAL SALT

Only a small percentage of salt produced is for domestic use. The vast majority produced worldwide since the late 18th and early 19th centuries has been used in chemical industries. These industries grew out of the previous work of alchemists who changed substances with water, mixed them together or studied the effects of heat on them.

Initially salt didn't seem to be very exciting, until someone discovered how to make hydrochloric acid from sulphuric acid and salt. Sulphuric acid and hydrochloric acid were used instead of buttermilk to provide a souring agent in the bleaching of textiles. In 1772 or 1773 a Swedish chemist called Carl Scheele managed to react hydrochloric acid with manganese dioxide to make chlorine. Chlorine was able to bleach products derived from vegetable matter, such as cotton. In 1785 a French chemist, Berthollet, used a solution of chlorine in alkali to make an industrial bleach. James Watt, who was a chemist before he got more interested in steam power, had been researching the production of alkali from the reaction of salt with lime and coal.

Early production of chlorine meant that you needed salt, sulphuric acid and manganese dioxide altogether at the point where you wanted to use the chlorine, which was not always convenient, but in 1790 Charles Tennant introduced ready-made bleaching powder in Glasgow. What was really still needed for the industry to develop further, however, was the production of alkali from salt. But salt tax was still in place and the government was unwilling to reduce this tax on the raw material for anything, even the advancement of science. They needed the money for the Napoleonic Wars. Watt and friends tried to change the government's mind, but to no avail.

James Kier tried to get round the problem by using potassium and sodium sulphate with nitric acid and lime to make soap. Although this avoided the salt tax, it was slow and gave a poor yield. Another attempt was made by Fordyce, a doctor and chemist, but was thwarted by the Board of Customs, as potash was involved and that was also taxed. The supplies of ash had declined and Europe was being deforested. Potash had to be imported from North America, Russia and Scandinavia.

THE LEBLANC PROCESS

The breakthrough came from France. Scheele's discovery had provided the first step in the race to make alkali. Louis XVI in France offered a prize for a method of producing alkali from sea salt. In 1791 Leblanc found the second step in the process by adding crushed limestone and coal to sodium sulphate. The coal (carbon) was oxidized to form carbon dioxide and the sulphate became sulphide, leaving the sodium carbonate and calcium sulphide, or black ash. By 1800 soda ash was being produced at the rate of 10,000 to 15,000 tons per year. Because sodium carbonate dissolves in water the soda ash was separated from the black ash by washing. This water was then evaporated to leave the sodium carbonate.

The end of the Napoleonic Wars brought stability. After a repeal of a tax on salt in Britain in 1824 the development was unstoppable and by 1870 the output of soda ash from Britain had reached 200,000 tons a year, more than all other countries put together. The price was environmental devastation. Sulphuric acid released hydrochloric acid gas into the atmosphere. For every 8 tons of soda ash produced, 7 tons of calcium sulphide waste hung around on the ground, smelling of rotten eggs. The surrounding land was scorched and fields and gardens produced little that was not spoiled. The people who worked in these factories or who lived close by must have suffered greatly. Luckily another process was invented without the major disadvantages. This was the Solvay process.

THE SOLVAY PROCESS

Ernest Solvay developed a method of bubbling carbon dioxide through brine mixed with ammonia to make sodium bicarbonate (baking soda). This could then be converted to soda ash by drying in a kiln. This was much cleaner and more efficient. The Leblanc process needed a large supply of white salt, whereas the Solvay process used brine, which saved a lot of production costs and evaporation processes.

ELECTROLYSIS OF BRINE

Over the years, soda and potash were defined as both natural and artificial products and as vegetable and mineral. Sir Humphry Davy decomposed both alkalies and called them sodium and potassium, which are really Latinized versions of soda and potash. The two metals cannot be isolated by normal chemical processes and were only prepared after the discovery of the electric current in 1800, when the electrolytic processes were developed. Davy's method was modified and called the Castner process. This produced chlorine, caustic soda and hydrogen on an industrial scale in the 1870s and was used to prepare sodium for a long time. Most is now prepared by the Down's process which produces chlorine as well as sodium.

DOWN'S PROCESS

This uses a carbon anode and iron cathode. The electrolyte sodium chloride has been fused to a liquid by heating. Sodium chloride is a poor conductor of electricity, but fusing it mobilizes the sodium and chloride ions, which then allow conduction of electric current. Some calcium chloride and sodium carbonate is added to reduce the temperature and to keep the electrolyte liquid at around 600°C (1112°F).

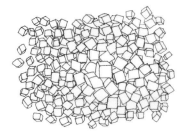

INDUSTRIAL USES TODAY

Passing an electrical current through a strong solution of salt in water causes electrolysis. Three products are formed:

- Chlorine (Cl_2)
- Hydrogen (H_2)
- Sodium hydroxide (NaOH)

Hydrogen and chlorine gases are explosive when mixed so they must be separated. All three chemicals are important useful products which can be combined to make a whole array of other chemicals and products.

CHEMICALS MADE FROM SODIUM CHLORIDE

CHLORINE
This is used primarily in producing polymers in the manufacture of plastics, synthetic fibres and synthetic rubber. It is also used in crude oil refining, for making pesticides and in household bleach, water and sewage treatment.

Demand for salt to produce chlorine chemicals is falling. Much of the decreased demand for chlorine has been attributed to environmental concerns about dioxins.

CHLORINE DIOXIDE
This form of chlorine is used for bleaching wood pulp and flour and for disinfecting water. Chlorine dioxide is used in many industrial water treatment applications including cooling towers, food processing and the control of the legionnaire bacteria.

SODIUM HYDROXIDE
More commonly known as caustic soda or lye, this is a main constituent of a range of more complex chemicals and used as a strong chemical base in laboratories and in the manufacture of pulp and paper, textiles, drinking water, soaps and detergents.

Sodium hydroxide is used domestically for unblocking drains. The chemical converts grease to a form of soap, producing a water-soluble form which can be dissolved by flushing. Strong drain cleaners are highly caustic and should be handled with care.

In the early 20th century it was used to relax or straighten the hair of people of African ethnicity, but because of the high incidence of chemical burns, chemical relaxer manufacturers started to use other alkaline chemicals.

Sodium hydroxide is used as a catalyst in the manufacture of biodiesel, a liquid fuel source largely compatible with petroleum-based diesel fuel. It replaces glycerol with a short chain alcohol such as methanol or ethanol. Waste vegetable oils can even be used, so the process is very 'green', generating a valuable fuel to combat pollution by carbon fuels.

Given the caustic nature of sodium hydroxide it is slightly surprising to note that food uses of lye include washing or chemical peeling of fruits and vegetables. It is also used in chocolate and cocoa processing, caramel colour production, poultry scalding, soft drink processing, and for thickening ice cream. Pretzels are glazed with it to make them brown and olives are often soaked in lye to soften them, while German lye rolls are glazed with a lye solution before baking to make them crisp.

SODIUM HYPOCHLORITE

Sodium hydroxide and chlorine combine to form sodium hypochlorite solution. When concentrated it is a strong oxidizer so is highly corrosive. It is used in dilute form of 3 to 6 per cent as domestic bleach. Commercially it is used in the dairy industry as a disinfectant. It is also used to chlorinate water.

SODIUM CHLORATE

Under different reaction conditions, sodium hydroxide and chlorine will react to form sodium chlorate. This is mostly used for bleaching paper and pulp and as a herbicide. Pretty nasty stuff, the white crystals can be highly explosive or inflammable if mixed with organic matter. Weedkillers contain about 53 per cent sodium chlorate. Poor plants!

HYDROGEN CHLORIDE

As we have already seen, when chlorine gas is burned in hydrogen, the two gases react to form hydrogen chloride. This dissolves in water to form hydrochloric acid. Made in this way it is very pure, and can be used safely in the food and pharmaceutical industries.

CALCIUM HYPOCHLORITE

Calcium hypochlorite, known as bleaching powder, is widely used for water treatment and as a bleaching agent for cotton and linen. This chemical is relatively stable and has greater chlorine available than sodium hypochlorite, which is liquid bleach. Calcium hypochlorite is used for the disinfection of drinking water or swimming pool water. It is also used in the manufacture of chloroform.

SODIUM SULPHATE (Glauber's salts)

Sodium sulphate has several important industrial uses. It is produced from naturally occurring sodium-sulphate-bearing brines or crystalline evaporite deposits and as a by-product from different chemical processes. Examples of these are the production of ascorbic acid, boric acid, cellulose, chromium chemicals, lithium carbonate, rayon, silica pigments, and battery acid recycling. Sodium sulphate is considered to be a waste product but has several important and useful applications in various products, such as in pulp and paper, soaps and detergents, and textiles.

Sodium sulphate summary:

- Batteries
- Cellulose
- Ceramics
- Detergents
- Dyes
- Pharmaceuticals
- Explosives
- Fertilizers
- Metal fluxes
- Paper
- Pharmaceuticals
- Rayon

- Photography
- Pigments
- Plating salts

- Rubber
- Soap
- Textiles

SODIUM PERCHLORATE

Perchlorate salts act as oxidizers in propellants such as rocket boosters. Sodium perchlorate is used in some pyrotechnics but is hygroscopic. It is made from sodium chloride with platinum anodes, or sometimes other metals are involved.

SODIUM BICARBONATE (bicarbonate of soda)

This common substance is used in textile manufacturing, processing leather, making soap and glass. It is also used for leavening food when baking and is the main constituent of baking powder. It is used for neutralizing acids and odours, and for cleaning. It should be part of anyone's store cupboard because it is so versatile. In fact there are so many uses, I have written a separate book on it!

SODIUM CARBONATE

More commonly known as soda ash or washing soda, this chemical is used in the manufacture of glass, pulp, paper and rayon. Its most important use is in the chemical make-up of glass. In chemistry it is often used as an electrolyte, as it acts as a very good conductor in the process of electrolysis. Sodium carbonate is widely used in photographic processes as a pH regulator for developing agents. In brick-making it is used as a wetting agent, and is used in some swimming pools to neutralize the acidic effects of chlorine and raise pH.

Domestically it is used to soften water during laundry and reduces the amount of detergent needed. It effectively removes oil, grease and alcohol stains, and is used as a de-scaling agent in boilers.

Here is a summary list of uses of sodium carbonate:

- Abrasives
- Adhesives
- Batteries
- Ceramics
- Cleansers
- Cosmetics
- De-scaler
- Degreasers
- Detergents
- Dyes
- Explosives
- Fats and oils
- Fertilizers
- Fire extinguishers
- Insecticides
- Leather
- Metal fluxes
- Ore refining
- Paint removers
- Paper
- Petroleum
- Pigments
- Soap
- Textiles
- Water softeners
- Wetting agent

SODIUM PEROXIDE

This is an oxidizing agent for bleaching paper, cloth, wood, ivory and for purifying the air in confined spaces such as submarines or aeroplanes.

HYDROCHLORIC ACID

This has been an important fundamental chemical since the Industrial Revolution. Applications include vinyl chloride, for PVC plastic, polyurethane, synthetic rubber and the cleaning of gas and oil wells. It is an element used in making glass, rayon, polyester and other synthetic fibres, leather processing, plastics, soaps and detergents. Other uses include household cleaning, many pharmaceutical products, and building construction. Oil production is sometimes stimulated by injecting hydrochloric acid into rock formations to dissolve rock. Nice!

Another slightly surprising application, to a novice like me, is its use in the food industry, such as in the production of gelatin and other food ingredients. Perhaps it helps to know that hydrochloric acid forms the majority of the human digestive fluid, gastric acid. Many chemical reactions involving hydrochloric acid are used in food additives such as fructose, citric acid, lysine and aspartame, my most feared additive. Yet another good reason for getting away from processed foods.

SODIUM NITRATE (Chile saltpetre)

This is an ingredient in fertilizers, rocket propellants and explosives. It was used extensively for the making of gunpowder towards the end of the 19th century. It also finds uses in the glass and pottery enamel industries.

Sodium nitrate is used as a food preservative and is found naturally in leafy green vegetables. It is believed to have health benefits by increasing oxygen supply to blood, as well as known health side effects at high doses. It is used in the curing of bacon and is found as an additive in hot dogs.

LIQUID SODIUM

This is used as a coolant, or heat exchanger, and is an essential element in the nuclear process. It is prepared by electrolysis of dry-fused sodium chloride. Liquid sodium is also used in medicine, agriculture and photography, in street lights, batteries and glass.

METALLIC SODIUM

In its metallic form sodium can be used to refine some reactive metals, such as zirconium and potassium, and is used in making brass, bronze and case-hardened steel. It is also used for fumigating materials and in indigo and other synthetic dyes. The largest use was once in leaded petrol and high-performance internal combustion engines. It is used as a heat transfer fluid in some types of nuclear reactors.

Sodium vapour lamps are an efficient means of producing light from electricity, often used for street lighting. Low-pressure sodium lamps give a distinctive yellow-orange light and high-pressure lamps give a more natural peach-coloured light.

Summary of sodium uses:

- Bactericides
- Case hardening
- Cosmetics
- Detergents
- Ore refining
- Dyes and fixation
- Flour conditioning
- Fumigation
- Heat transfer
- Pulp bleaching

- Organic synthesis
- Paints
- Pharmaceuticals
- Photography
- Pigments
- Plating salts

- Starch conversion
- Tetraethyl lead
- Textile bleaching
- Titanium metal
- Zirconium metal

SOAP MANUFACTURE

The most common early soaps were made from potash and pearl ash. Early references to the use of soap include the Babylonians, about 2800 BC, and the Phoenicians, *c*.600 BC. The Egyptians used natron, and the Spaniards and other Mediterranean people, were using burned seaweed to provide the alkali they needed. Early uses included the cleaning of wool and cotton fibre prior to spinning and weaving.

Soap is basically a reaction between fatty acids and an alkali. When fats or oils are mixed with a strong alkali the fats are split into fatty acids and glycerine. The sodium or potassium in the alkali joins with the fatty acid as the basis of soap.

The three main stages of early soap-making were:

- Making a wood ash solution called lye.
- Cleaning the fats.
- Boiling the fats with the lye to make soap.

Early manufacturers obtained the lye from putting potash into a bottomless barrel over a stone slab, resting on rocks. Straw or sticks were put in the bottom as a sort of sieve. By slowly pouring water over the ashes you could produce the lye, a brown liquid dripping down into a container below. This could then be used with the rendered-down fat to produce soap. When wood supplies dwindled towards the end of the 18th century, pearl ash manufacturing started to decline, making way for more commercial methods. The Leblanc process changed soap-making for ever. Sodium alkalis made harder, better soap without the necessity to add salt.

SOAP AND GLYCERINE MANUFACTURE

Fats and oils are heated with caustic soda to produce soap and glycerine. The continuous process, developed in about 1940, means, as the name suggests, that production can continue without making batches. Soap takes about six hours to make nowadays. Previously, by the 'kettle process', it took 4 to 11 days to complete a batch.

Soap and glycerine are produced as the fat reacts with alkali after boiling. To separate the soap and glycerine, salt is added, causing the soap to rise to the top and the glycerine to settle to the bottom. A second step to remove small amounts of fat that have not turned to soap may involve the use of caustic soda (which is also made from salt), followed by a second salt treatment.

Glycerine is used to make hand lotion, drugs and nitroglycerine, the main component of explosives such as dynamite.

Sodium sulphate is used to make soaps and detergents. It is an especially important ingredient in powdered soaps, although not as much is needed to make liquid soaps.

GLASS-MAKING

The most important chemical activity was the making of alkali. When mixed with lime and sand it could be used to make glass. Worldwide, synthetic production of alkali is about 22 million metric tons, about twice that of natural production. Most of this soda ash is used to make chemicals and glass.

NATRON AND GLASS-MAKING

Glass-makers didn't wait for the invention of the Leblanc process. People had been making glass since before 2200 BC in Iran and the Egyptians were able to make coloured glass. Roman technology used glass for more practical purposes than just for decoration and used semi-precious stones to give different colours. For example, turquoise gave a pale blue glass, and fluorite a purple hue. It was manufactured by melting alkali (potash or sodium) with silica such as quartz or sand.

During the next several hundred years, glass developed in different ways in various parts of the world, and was based on either soda or potash. The soda was found in Mediterranean regions in the ashes of plants in salty sea marshes and in seaweed. Germany and Bohemia used potash from beechwood and France used bracken as a source. The quality of the glass depended on the preparation of the soda.

Lead glass or flint glass was invented in the 17th century, in the days of William and Mary of Orange, in the Netherlands. This could be cut to enhance designs and show off its sheen. After this, there were still more changes and refinements to glass and its production; for example, large amounts of lead were used with potash and Venetian glass was produced with soda. Flint glass was made from three parts sand, two parts red lead and one part potash or pearl ash from Canada or Russia.

The Leblanc process made alkali easier and cheaper to make and therefore glass-making developed at a faster rate. Europe seemed to have the monopoly on expensive and decorative blown glassware until an unknown carpenter in Massachusetts, USA, invented a new method of pressed glass in 1827. Then, in 1864 in Western Virginia, William Leighton brought about a revolution in the process of making glass at a fraction of the price of the lead and flint varieties. His pressed glass was of equally good clarity and could be produced thinly by being pressed into a mould. The major difference, though, was the use of sodium bicarbonate and lime instead of lead. All this and manufactured at a third of the price, because the bicarbonate of soda was readily available in large quantities.

SODA-LIME GLASS
Nowadays, 90 per cent of commercial glass is produced in this, the least expensive way of making glass. Soda-lime glass is primarily used for bottles, jars, everyday drinking glasses and window glass.

Soda-lime glass contains approximately:

- 60—75% silica
- 12—18% soda
- 5—12% lime

Soda-lime glass is not resistant to high temperatures, sudden thermal changes, or to corrosive chemicals

Using bicarbonate of soda for commercial production of glass has several benefits. It is effective at high temperatures of around +400°C. During manufacture the glass gives off acid fumes and dust. Bicarbonate of soda neutralizes acid components of gases so that they can be discharged into the atmosphere. The residual chemicals of sodium sulphate are recycled in the furnace, also using bicarbonate of soda.

LEATHER CURING AND TANNING

If you are vegetarian you'll probably want to skip this section and move on. I wouldn't blame you!

The processing of animal hides for making leather has changed little since primitive man started to use it. Unless they were treated, the skins used for clothes, footwear, water carrying and many other things would have rotted. Drying skins preserved them, but resulted in a very hard, uncomfortable material.

Curing protected and softened the skins and made them waterproof. Several methods have evolved.

DRYING
Chilling or refrigeration requires no chemical additions, but before this was available skins were laid out on stones in the sun to dry. This method is the oldest form of curing, but there is very little control on speed of drying and it is liable to cause problems later on during the tanning process. Stretching the skins on frames and drying in the shade was a better method, but not as good as brining.

BRINING

Washed skins or hides are put into a salt solution and kept moving constantly, until the brine penetrates the skins. The concentration of salt is kept high, by continually adding salt to the brine solution and a disinfectant. The skins are then taken out and dried ready for shipping or further processing. This is a good but expensive method for preserving skins. It is more common than wet-salting, as it's considered a faster, easier method. It takes 10–16 hours before the skins are completely cured and ready to move on to the next stage.

WET-SALTING

Skins are placed in a pile with salt sprinkled on top of each addition to the pile, until there are about 50 skins. The salt absorbs the moisture from the skins and the resulting brine penetrates the skins, killing off the bacteria. Once the hides are in this state, they will keep for a very long time, as long as temperature and humidity are controlled.

DRY-SALTING

This involves wet-salting as a first stage before the hides are hung up to dry. Dry-salting reduces the chance of heat damage and brings down transport costs.

PICKLING

This is a method most commonly used with sheepskins. The skins are kept damp and cool (below 20°C, 68°F) in a salt and acid solution.

THE START OF THE TANNING PROCESS

If you are still reading this section, well done! Having researched this topic, I know why I never considered the medical world as a career. I'm not normally squeamish and I do wear leather shoes, but there is a limit. You don't really need to know some of the details, so I've only included the first stages of tanning, where salt products are used.

SOAKING

The first operation is to soak the skins. This is done to reverse the curing process and to remove dirt and nasty bits. Soaking takes place in big drums, firstly with water and then with detergent, salt and a biocide (usually chlorine-based) being added. The process continues until the water remains clean and the skins have been rehydrated. This may take from 18 to 72 hours.

LIMING

The cleaned skins still have their hair on which must be removed completely with the root hairs and epidermis. Sodium sulphide or sodium hydrosulphide is added to the soaked skins for about an hour until they do their job. Let's leave it there. Salt doesn't feature in the remainder of the process.

PULP AND PAPER-MAKING

In paper-making, caustic soda is used to process wood fibres. Chlorine is used to bleach the pulp, but sodium chlorate, also made from salt, is replacing chlorine as the primary chemical for bleaching pulp.

The following chemicals derived from salt are used in pulp and paper production:

- Sodium sulphate (salt cake), for recovering other chemicals.
- Sodium carbonate (soda ash), as above.
- Sodium hydrosulphite, for bleaching.
- Sodium silicate, for deinting, i.e. cleaning waste paper for recycling.
- Sodium hydroxide, for pulping.
- Chlorine dioxide, for pulp bleaching.
- Chlorine, for water treatment.

Emulsified sulphur and sodium hydroxide can be used in place of sodium sulphate in paper production.

FOOD INDUSTRIES

FARMING

Rock salt is sometimes scattered on grass to make it more appetizing for beef cattle. They eat more and gain weight. In sugar beet production rock salt is used to fertilize the soil with sodium. This makes sugar beet yield more sugar.

CURING FISH

Methods of curing fish by drying, salting, smoking or pickling have been employed since ancient times. Before the days of refrigeration, fishing boats used brine or dry salt to keep fish from rotting. Salting and drying made the fish very hard so it would keep for a long time. Sometimes fish was packed fresh in barrels of salt.

The swifter boats of today and the use of refrigeration mean that most fish are now brought ashore unsalted. Fish to be cured are usually first cleaned and scaled before being packed between layers of salt or immersed in brine. The most commonly salted fish are cod, herring, mackerel and haddock. Kippers are split herring, and bloaters are whole, salted, smoked herring. Sardines, pilchards and anchovies are all fish of the herring family, often salted and smoked before they are preserved in oil. Fish are dried under controlled conditions of temperature, humidity and air velocity.

In Norway, there used to be five different grades of salt cod. The best grade was called superior extra. Superior klippfisk is salted fresh, whereas the cheaper grades might be frozen first. Lower grades are salted by injecting a salt-water solution into the fish. The superior grade is dried twice, much like Parma ham. Between the two drying sessions, the fish rests and the flavour matures.

You can find some recipes and methods of curing fish in the Cooking with Salt section.

MEAT CURING

Ham
The word *prosciutto* means 'thoroughly dried' although it means ham in Italian. Raw ham is cured ham which has not been cooked. Making cured ham can take from nine to eighteen months, depending on the size of the ham, which is first cleaned, salted with sea salt and left for a couple of months. During this time it is squeezed in a press to drain out any blood left in the meat. Next it is washed several times to remove the salt, after which it is hung in a cool, airy place. In some places the ham is smoked by burning different types of wood to give a special flavour. The ham is then left to dry for a varying amount of time, depending on the weight and the climate.

Prosciutto is never cured with sodium nitrate or potassium nitrate, which are normally used in other hams to produce a rosy pink colour. Prosciutto's characteristic pigmentation seems to be produced by certain bacteria, rather than a direct chemical reaction.

Bacon
Bacon is made from fresh pork which has been preserved with salt so that it will keep for longer. There are two main methods of curing:

Dry Curing
From Saxon times pigs were fattened on acorns in oak forests during autumn and the meat cured to provide food for the family in winter months. Bacon formed part of the rations for long distance sea journeys.

Wet Curing
This method immerses the meat in a liquid solution of salt and saltpetre, containing useful salt-tolerant bacteria, for three to four days. This provides a milder form of curing in the brine under refrigeration. As meat keeps fresh longer at lower temperatures it does not require so much salt. This was developed in the 1840s in Wiltshire. As there were no refrigerators back then the roof was packed with winter ice to lower the temperature.

Nowadays curing is usually carried out by dissolving salt to form a strong brine to act as a pickle. In many cases the pickle is pumped into the meat to speed up the process, as in the case of bacon and ham. Yield is increased by the addition of water. The salt for these purposes is refined and of high quality.

See Cooking with Salt for some methods and ideas.

BREAD AND PASTRY
Salt is used to give added flavour to bread and pastry. Salt performs a function in controlling the rate at which the yeast works in the dough, giving a better texture. It is almost impossible to make bread without adding salt.

CANNING OF MEAT AND VEGETABLES
Salt is added to the products during processing. Many vegetable products are packed in brine, which should be washed out before reheating.

CHEESE MANUFACTURE
Salting is a vital part of the cheese-making process and serves four purposes:

- To slow down the development of bacteria at the beginning of the cheese-making process. These bacteria aid the formation of the curds and whey. Unchecked they would cause the cheese to spoil very quickly.
- Salt acts as a preservative in the cheese-making process. This is important in making hard cheese that will keep a long time, like Cheddar.
- It slows down the growth of undesirable bacteria.
- Salt acts as a flavour enhancer. If the cheese does not have salt it cannot mature and would quickly become inedible.

Most cheese today is made on automatic machines and salting must be carried out in a continuous process. The salt used must be extremely dry at all times. I remember visiting a cheese farm in Normandy some years ago, producing Neufchatel cheese. I was amazed to see the half-ready cheese being rolled in salt before being left in a cool room for the bacterial moulds (or 'mushrooms', as they were translated) to finish the process.

Again, you can find out more about cheese and salt in the recipe and health sections.

OTHER INDUSTRIES AND USES OF SALT

TEXTILE INDUSTRIES
Salt is used to standardize dye batches. Salt is added to the dye baths during the process to make the dyes fast. Flossy salt is the grade most commonly used in this process. Sodium sulphate is also used in the textile industry.

METAL PROCESSING
Salt is used in metal processing and secondary aluminium, making to remove impurities. Salt is used as a flux. The salt sits on top of the molten aluminium in molten form, removing iron and other metals and leaving pure metal.

RUBBER
Rubber manufacturers use salt to separate rubber from latex. Synthetic rubber is produced in the form of white latex to which salt is added as an emulsifier. Medium quality, unrefined salt is used for this purpose.

CERAMICS
Salt is used to vitrify or fire the surface of heated clays. Ceramics are formed at temperatures above 800°C (1472°F). This process is called vitrification.

Salt is used to form the very smooth glaze on clay tiles or pottery ware. After a kiln of tiles reaches a white heat, salt is fed on to the fire. The salt vaporizes and passes on to the surface of the tile, forming a glass film.

OIL AND GAS DRILLING
Drillers working on muds use salt to prevent fermentation, increase density and to stabilize drilling in rock salt formations. Salt is used to mix with boring

mud (yes, mud is boring isn't it?) which is pumped down bore holes. This forms a wall when drilling through gravel or sandy material, which would otherwise not stand up on its own.

DRY CLEANING
Salt is used in dry-detergent processes.

WATER SOFTENING
Salt is used in both industrial and home water-softening units. Salt for this purpose is usually a washed or refined grade. A similar type of salt is used for making a brine for brine cooling systems.

FREEZING POINT DEPRESSANT
Salt finds its way into making coal antifreeze, highway de-icing, ice manufacture, iron ore antifreeze, refrigerating brines and refrigerating cars.

DE-ICING ROADS
Salt is the major de-icer used around the world. Some other salts, such as calcium chloride and potassium chloride, can be used but these options are more expensive than salt. Due to the limitless supply available, salt is not likely to be replaced in most of its industrial and domestic uses. We'll just have to put up with the damage to metal and road surfaces caused by the salt, in exchange for its ability to melt ice.

LENSES AND PRISMS
Sodium chloride is used for windows, lenses and prisms. Because of its low absorption, sodium chloride is being used in high-power laser systems. It can be used at temperatures up to 400°C (752°F).

RENEWABLE ENERGY
Salt domes produce heat which may be used as a source of renewable energy, either by developing and using this energy directly or by making electricity from the heat.

Molten salt solar energy production

Systems using molten salt as thermal media have been proposed for solar thermal power generation and for synthetic fuel production. Research is progressing in California and in Japan.

Salt gradient solar ponds

Solar ponds are an inexhaustible source of renewable energy, given the right conditions. A salt gradient solar pond operates using layers of different concentrations of salinity to trap heat so it can be recovered. There are three distinct layers of water in the pond. The top layer has a low salt content whereas the bottom layer has a high salt content. The middle layer acts as an insulation that prevents heat exchange. A solar pond can be used for various applications, such as process heating, sea water desalination, refrigeration, drying and generating solar power. There are many ponds operating throughout the world, largely in developing countries, where large collectors can be set up with clay or plastic pond liners at low cost.

MOLTEN SALT WASTE INCINERATION

This is a way of dealing with unwanted 'energetic' materials that cannot be easily recycled. Open burning, detonation and incineration have been the most commonly used in the past but this method may provide a more environmentally friendly means of destroying materials from conventional and nuclear weapons.
The process involves a crucible of molten salt in which high explosives and propellants are reduced to carbon dioxide, nitrogen and water.

SALT-BATH FURNACE

This is a liquid-bath furnace in which the heating medium is a molten salt material. Salt-bath furnaces are used for heat treating, brazing, and tempering steel.

Salt: Kill or Cure?

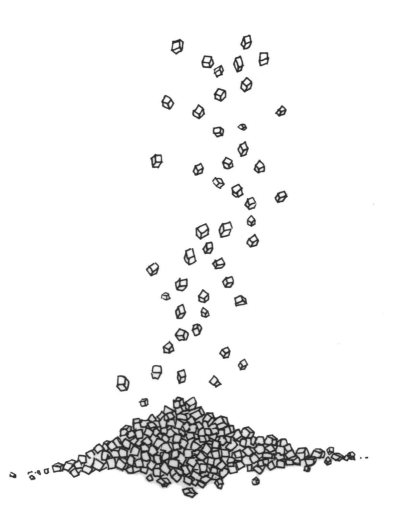

PHYSIOLOGICAL NEED FOR SALT

Sodium chloride is a vital constituent in all living creatures. It is essential for the functions and processes of all animals, including human beings. All of our tissues and body fluids contain salt. Tears are salty and when you sweat, or gently perspire if you are a genteel person, you are losing salt through the pores of your skin, as your body cools down. Salt helps to regulate the water content of the body and is replaced by natural or added salt in your food and also when you add it as a condiment at the table. A normal body contains about a third of the quantity of salt there is in sea water. It has been suggested that the need for salt has come from the days when animal life first emerged from the oceans, which reminds me of a memorable beer advertisement that retraced the steps of mankind from shore to pub.

As we saw earlier, when early man was a hunter he got all the salt he needed from animals, if he managed to catch any, that is. The alternatives were shellfish and other aquatic sources, like fish. As more pastoral activities like farming took over and omnivorous humans learned to love grains and plants to eat, there was a greater need for salt, both for humans themselves and for their animals.

LOW-SALT DIETS
It is interesting to note that among isolated groups of people discovered around the world over the course of time, required intake of salt is low, if not non-existent. Sodium and chlorine, the two components of salt, are both necessary for survival, but that doesn't mean to say we need to eat them together as salt. Many parts of equatorial Africa do not have huge salt reserves because of the igneous rocks that dominate and the only salt is to be found in rain or dust. Here, plants and insects exist that are able to capitalize on minute quantities of chlorides and concentrate them. People have, in the past, survived by drinking the blood and urine of animals that have collected and concentrated the salt in their blood by feeding on large quantities of plants.

The Yanomami Indians, who live in the Amazon in South America, are hunters, fishermen and cultivators of plantains and cassava in forest clearings. The people eat a diet that is very low in salt. They have the lowest blood pressure readings measured and there is no obesity or consumption of alcohol. Studies of the Yanomami have provided scientists with valuable insights into the link between hypertension and consumption of sodium. Their blood pressure does not increase with age, unlike in most countries.

Indigenous hunters in Greenland did not eat salt until they were introduced to it in the 17th century by Europeans, who were whaling. Like our ancestors, Lapps, Samoyeds, Bedouin, Masai and Zulus used to consume all the sodium they needed from the animals and fish they ate. There is no doubt that early settlements grew up around brine springs. These were probably discovered by following animals to their salt licks.

SALT DEFICIENCY

Tribes like the Masai believe that cattle are too precious and valuable to kill, so daily nourishment is received by bleeding live cattle by opening a vein on the neck or flank with the point of an arrow. The blood is collected and often mixed with fresh or curdled milk and in this way salt is included in the daily diet.

Salt deprivation has its problems for health and well-being and it has been suggested that, just as salt-starved animals eat part of their litter in order to stay alive, extreme salt hunger is one of the causes of cannibalism. Women of the Suya people in the Amazon collect water hyacinth or pond lilies, dry them in the sun and burn their leaves. The ash is then passed through a kind of grass filter to obtain a potassium chloride salt, or potash. This is not the same as sodium chloride and is too rich in potassium to make a good salt, but it avoids salt deficiency.

Aborigines in New Guinea have been observed making secret expeditions to the sea coast to put sea water into hollow bamboos which are carried back to their tribe. A long walk for a little salt, but if you don't have a lot of salt in your diet, you don't miss it.

SODIUM AND CHLORINE

As we have seen, sodium is a component of salt. In 2.5 grams of salt there is 1 gram of sodium. Sodium is a component of other ingredients, as described previously. Sodium bicarbonate used in baking and monosodium glutamate used as a flavour enhancer are two examples, but we'll come back to the latter one shortly. Too much sodium in the diet can lead to health problems, such as high blood pressure (hypertension). This in turn substantially increases the risk of developing heart disease or stroke.

FUNCTIONS OF SODIUM

Sodium is a must in our diet and is an element the body cannot manufacture itself. Many functions are regulated by sodium which is contained in body fluids transporting oxygen and nutrients. Sodium also regulates the balance of fluids in the body that deliver the nutrients, the fluid volume and the balance of acids. The average salinity of blood and other body fluids is 0.9 per cent. An adult human body contains about 250 grams (9 oz) of salt. Any excess is automatically disposed of.

In addition to controlling fluids, sodium facilitates the transmission of nerve impulses. Like potassium, calcium and magnesium, sodium is an electrolyte, regulating the electrical charges moving around cells in the body.

Sodium controls some of the senses, which would otherwise be dulled. For example, it is necessary for signals to reach and return from the brain. It regulates taste, smell and touch processes. Sodium ions are essential for the contraction of muscles. Of course, the biggest muscle of all and the most vital of these is the heart. So, you might think, a little extra salt can only do you good if we need it to function properly, but that's where we go wrong.

FUNCTIONS OF CHLORIDE

Like sodium, chloride is essential to good health as well. It is a must in the digestion process, where it preserves the acid-base balance in the body. Chloride helps the body to absorb potassium. It supplies the basis of the hydrochloric acid in the stomach's gastric juices. These help to break down and digest the food we eat, and control levels of bacteria in the stomach. Another function of chloride is to help the blood carry carbon dioxide back from tissues to the lungs.

KEEPING THE BALANCE

A little is good, but too much is bad. The balance needs to be upheld. This is why patients who are dehydrated by vomiting or extreme diarrhoea are given saline drips. These are a weak solution of salt and liquid nutrients fed into the body via a blood vessel, when the patient is too ill to eat or drink normally. People suffering from drought and starvation in Third World countries, or after disasters, are given salt and sugar solutions to help rehydration.

Living in a hot climate means you sweat more, so you lose more salt through loss of fluid. In the same way, a good workout in the gym or on an athletics track will get your heart pumping and your sweat glands working overtime to cool you down. Some athletes take salt tablets to relieve the effects of muscle cramps, brought on by the loss of fluids and salt, but these are not normally necessary for everyday life. Sodium requirements are linked closely to water needs. If you drink more water you will replace the losses without the need for extra salt. One exception to this were coalminers, who were given salt tablets to take in the extremely hot conditions tolerated daily when working underground under great physical stress. These salt tablets were added to the miners' metal water carriers, known in some mining areas including the Kent coalfield, as Dudleys.

People who suffer from kidney problems and very young children can't take high levels of sodium because the kidneys can't excrete the excess. It is very important, therefore, that salt is never added to baby food.

HEALTH PROBLEMS

HIGH BLOOD PRESSURE
The link to high blood pressure or hypertension has already been referred to, although consuming high levels of sodium is not the only cause of high blood pressure. There are often no symptoms of hypertension, but over-consumption increases the risk of heart disease and stroke. It is recommended that the most effective diet to prevent or treat high blood pressure is one which is low in fat and sodium, and includes low-fat dairy products and plenty of fresh fruit and vegetables. Other factors, such as keeping physically active, not smoking and maintaining a healthy body weight, are also important in preventing hypertension. You can't do much if it is genetic, other than maintain a healthy and active lifestyle.

It has been estimated that about 18 million people in the UK have high blood pressure. The risk of developing heart disease or having a stroke is three times higher than for people with normal blood pressure. Nearly 238,000 people die each year from heart disease in the UK and around 50,000 people a year die from stroke. Lowering salt consumption seems to be, therefore, an important priority. There are variations. Statistically, among people of Afro-Caribbean origin living in the UK, up to 50 per cent over the age of 40 are likely to have high blood pressure compared to other ethnic groups. Stroke is also more common in Afro-Caribbean people. People of Pakistani, Bangladeshi and Chinese origin appear to have a lower risk.

A diet that is healthy doesn't have to be restricted to a particular need or symptom, especially when there might not be any outward symptoms for several years, before a condition is diagnosed. In any event, it makes sense to eat healthily, and without salt to cover up other flavouring in food you can identify other, more subtle flavours. In my experience, when you give up eating lots of salt, you find that processed food begins to taste even more salty, almost to the point of being inedible.

KIDNEY PROBLEMS
Our kidneys filter and clean the blood and get rid of waste products by making urine. They also regulate the amount of fluid we have in our bodies and the sodium levels and other salts. If these levels are too low, a hormone is released and this increases the amount of sodium held in the body by reducing the amount lost in urine. Regulation of fluid helps to regulate blood pressure as well. If the kidneys don't work properly, there will be changes in blood pressure and in the fluid balance of the body, leading to swelling, especially in the feet and ankles. More severe kidney problems will lead to a build-up of waste products in the blood, which the body cannot get rid of. It is very important to identify kidney disease at an early stage, especially among people with heart disease, hypertension or diabetes, and that is why these conditions are closely monitored, once identified. Treatment may be through a limited diet, to cut out high levels of potassium, sodium or phosphate and high protein foods and so limit the build-up of waste products.

CARDIAC ENLARGEMENT
Left ventricular hypertrophy is the thickening of the muscle of the left ventricle of the heart. It is frequently seen as a symptom of heart disease, although it can occur naturally as a reaction to aerobic exercise and strength training. High blood pressure can also be a cause.

STOMACH CANCER
A study a few years ago suggested that people who eat a high salt diet have a higher risk of stomach cancer. Research was carried out in Japan, where consumption of salt is high. Highly salted pickled food is popular and rates of stomach cancer are high. Nearly 40,000 men and women between 40 and 59 were followed over an 11-year period, measuring their daily salt intake. Researchers found that men who ate less than 6 grams of salt a day had a risk of 1 in 1,000 of developing stomach cancer. This risk went up to 1 in 500 for men eating 12—15 grams a day. Women faired a little better: those who ate less than 6 grams of salt a day had a risk factor of 1 in 2,000, but the risk rose to 1 in 1,300 for those who ate 12—15 grams a day. Eating high levels of salt is thought to waste the stomach lining.

In the UK the rate of stomach cancer has been falling over the last 70 years or so, making it the sixth most common cancer. One theory for this fall is that people in Britain have been eating less salted, smoked and pickled foods, as refrigeration has become the main way of preserving food. Cancer of the stomach is more common in older people. Nine out of ten people diagnosed with stomach cancer are over the age of 55.

OSTEOPOROSIS

Oh, the joys of getting older. Osteoporosis is a bone-wasting disease costing the NHS millions of pounds and causing disability in the elderly, especially women. The greatest risk factors for osteoporosis are poor diet in childhood and adolescence, when the bones are being formed. Also, the rate of bone loss in later life can be affected by other changes, such as hormone imbalances, speeding up the loss of calcium. Researchers now believe that eating too much salt can raise the blood pressure and that this also speeds up the body's loss of calcium. Measurements of over 3,600 women over three and a half years led the researchers to conclude that post-menopausal women with higher blood pressure had greater and faster loss of bone minerals than those with lower blood pressure. Smoking also increased the bone loss.

Bone loss over many years can lead to osteoporosis. Research shows hypertensive people excrete higher amounts of calcium in their urine than those with low blood pressure. Potassium helps to reduce calcium loss, whereas sodium speeds up the process, so, yet again, a low salt diet may save you from pain and suffering later in life. It is interesting to note that our diet today tends to be low in potassium and high in sodium. Potassium lowers blood pressure as well. Food processing tends to lower the potassium levels in many foods while increasing the sodium content, so, by cutting out a lot of the processed foods and eating potassium-rich fruit and vegetables, we can all do ourselves no end of good by lowering the blood pressure and delaying the onset of osteoporosis. By the way, men suffer from this disease as well. Many people seem to think it is only little old ladies who suffer.

OEDEMA

Oedema, or fluid retention, can be caused by eating highly salted food, and is more likely to occur when you get older. Cutting down your salt intake will help to reduce fluid retention, and patients who already have heart, kidney or liver problems will particularly benefit from cutting salt intake.

MENIERE'S DISEASE

This is a condition associated with vertigo, fluctuating hearing loss and tinnitus. Studies have shown in patients suffering from frequent attacks of vertigo that a change to a very low salt diet will lessen the frequency and severity of attacks measured over the period of a fortnight.

RECOMMENDED DAILY INTAKE OF SALT

Nowadays, most people eat more salt than they should. The recommended maximum amount for an adult is 6 grams of salt a day. This is the equivalent of taking 2.5 grams of sodium a day. It has been estimated that the average adult intake of salt is nearer to 9.5 grams a day, equivalent to about two teaspoonfuls of salt, or 3.7 grams of sodium. Children need less, but with the popularity of salty snack foods over the past couple of decades the amount of salt consumed by younger people has certainly not decreased.

Recommended salt intake per age group:

Age	Grams per day
Adult (over 15 years)	6
7—14 years	5
1—6 years	2
7—12 months	1
0—6 months	Less than 1 gram

UNDERSTANDING LABELS

First of all you have to understand the terms sodium and salt on food labels. Manufacturers don't have to give information unless a claim is made for nutritional value, but most manufacturers do so. If nutritional information is given, it has to be as sodium, not as salt. This is because it is the sodium that matters and because other additives contain sodium, apart from salt. These include monosodium glutamate, my personal horror 'flavour enhancer' additive, sodium saccharin (a sweetener), sodium ascorbate (an antioxidant) and sodium bicarbonate. Sodium is also found in some medicinal products, e.g. antacids. Chemical preservatives, such as sodium nitrite, sodium benzoate, sodium propionate, sodium citrate and sodium phosphate, contain small amounts of salt.

Read the labels

I've been reading food labels for a long time. I'd been aware of the salt and sugar added to baby foods and other foods when my children were growing up in the 1980s. One of the best interactive homework activities I ever set was for my class of primary pupils to go home and look at the baked beans in their cupboards. The sheer variety of products was astonishing, and the nutritional information most informative. We studied comparisons of contents in terms of food groups, energy and value for money. Some of the brands, usually but not always the cheapest, contained very high salt levels. It was a good exercise for all of us, adults and children. Tinned soups provide another eye-opener.

In the last few years I've developed high blood pressure and Type 2 diabetes, despite the fact that I've always watched our salt and sugar intake and I'm not obese. Nowadays, nearly all the food we eat at home is unprocessed or home grown. Having the odd treat of a meal out or a takeaway can send my body into a feeling I can only describe as like suffering from a mild hangover, even though I haven't overindulged. A tin of soup or a piece of blue cheese in isolation is okay, but the dreaded monosodium glutamate of a Chinese meal will give me the whole hangover feeling, even without any alcohol. Many people associate diabetes with only being about sugar intake, but there's a lot more to it than that. As a list of processed food containing sodium shows, there's a great deal of it about, so not adding salt to food at the table is only the tip of the iceberg. It's all the salt in the food already bought which causes the problems. High sodium foods don't always taste salty!

As well as reading labels you have the choice of reduced salt or low salt products and there is a big difference between the two.

REDUCED-SALT PRODUCTS

Food labelled as 'reduced salt or sodium' may indicate a lower salt content but it is still important to check food labels. Guidelines suggest that products labelled 'reduced salt' or 'reduced sodium' should contain at least 25 per cent less than the standard product. The baked beans I've been buying for the last 25 years are a reduced sugar and reduced salt type. The label information gives the following:

COMPARISON TABLE

Standard beans per 100 g	Reduced salt/sugar beans
Sugars 5.2 g	Sugars 3.2 g
Sodium 0.4 g	Sodium 0.2 g

Fine, that's within the 25 per cent reduction, but that's only per 100, about half a portion per ½ can, i.e. one serving.

Carbohydrates	26.5 g
Of which sugars	6.7 g
Of which starch	19.8 g
Salt	1.0 g
Of which sodium	0.4 g

So, I'm still eating a whole gram of salt in one healthy helping of high fibre (6.7 grams), protein filled (9.5 grams) portion, when only 49 per cent of the product is beans. Slightly confusing and surprising, isn't it? I'm going for the low salt in future.

LOW-SALT PRODUCTS
Food labelled as low salt or low sodium needs to have no more than 40 milligrams sodium per 100 grams or 100 millilitres.

SALT-FREE PRODUCTS
Salt or sodium free products must have no more than 5 milligrams sodium per 100 grams or 100 millilitres.

LOW-SODIUM ALTERNATIVES TO SALT
There are many products around these days that are labelled as low in sodium, so you might think that the answer is just to use one of these in the same quantities as before, liberally sprinkling your fish and chips or whatever. Just remember that most of the salt you are going to eat is already there, in the batter, in the ketchup or other sauce and possibly the chip coating as well.

Salt substitutes vary in their composition, but their main ingredient is always potassium chloride. As I said earlier, potassium is an alternative, but shouldn't be used by some people on various medications or by those suffering from kidney problems. Even where the main ingredient is potassium chloride, there will still be between 20 per cent and 33 per cent sodium chloride in the low salt brand, plus an anti-caking agent, such as magnesium carbonate.

CALCULATING THE SALT

To convert sodium to salt intake on packages, if only the sodium content is shown, you need to do a quick calculation. Salt is about 40 per cent sodium, so if you multiply the content figure by 2.5 you will be able to work out the salt content. Also, remember that the figure will probably be given per 100 grams, so you need to consider the size of the portion as well.

Example: sodium content 0.8 g x 2.5 = 2 g of salt

The Food Standards Agency suggests the following categories for ready-made or processed food:

'a lot of' = 0.5 grams of sodium or more
per 100 grams of food
'a little' = 0.1 grams or less per 100 grams

TRAFFIC LIGHT LABELS

The newer food labels used by some supermarkets and manufacturers have 'traffic light' colours on the front of the pack. I find these very useful as they show you, at a glance, if a food is high (red), medium (amber) or low (green) in salt, sugar, fat and saturated fat. This is much easier to my mind than reaching for the reading glasses in the middle of the supermarket and reading the small print.

High or **red** means that you can eat small amounts, or just occasionally.

Medium or **amber** means that it is OK most of the time.

Low or **green** means a healthier choice.

This is fine unless you have a particularly strict diet or need to avoid a particular ingredient altogether.

SOME SURPRISING HIDDEN SALT

On average, 75 per cent of the salt in our diet comes from processed foods, although people eating more processed foods have even more. A further 10—15 per cent comes from salt added when cooking. Salt found naturally in foods represents the remaining 10 per cent. Such foods are whole grains, meat and dairy products which contain traces of sodium.

As well as being used as a flavour enhancer and preservative in processed food, salt has also been used as a binder, a fermentation control agent in breadmaking, as a colour enhancer and to add texture. The following processed foods all contain plenty of salt:

- Biscuits (cookies)
- Bread
- Butter and spreads
- Cakes
- Canned and packet soups
- Canned vegetables and baked beans
- Cheese
- Crisps (potato chips), salted nuts and snack foods
- Ham, sausages, bacon and other meat products
- Olives
- Pastries
- Pizza
- Pork pies
- Ready meals
- Smoked fish
- Some breakfast cereals

Some foods contain higher amounts of salt than you might expect.

Soup

A recent survey of nearly 600 brands of soup showed that almost half had more than the recommended levels of salt (0.6 grams per 100 grams). The average was 1.6 grams per serving. 20 per cent had over 2 grams of salt, which is a third of the recommended daily intake for an adult. Hmm, that doesn't seem to make soup a healthy option, unless you read labels carefully or make your own.

Sandwiches
A jam sandwich has only 30 per cent less salt than a vegemite or marmite sandwich. Most of the salt comes from the bread.

Cereals
A bowl of cornflakes may have about the same salt content as a small packet of plain crisps (US potato chips).

Biscuits
Some sweet biscuits (cookies) contain as much or more salt than savoury biscuits, although they don't taste very salty because the sugar masks the taste.

Other salts
Sea salt, onion, celery or garlic salts are not low sodium substitutes.

Fatty spreads
Ordinary mayonnaise has the most salt (240 mg/100 g), followed by margarine (140 mg), butter (130 mg) and cream cheese (85 mg).

Soft drinks and mineral water
Salt is sometimes used to cover up a metallic or chemical aftertaste in soft drinks. Some mineral waters contain sodium and the amount they contain can vary quite a lot. This depends on the mix of mineral and the source of the water. There are no limits on the amount of sodium a mineral water can contain, so you need to read the labels. Spring water and table water are controlled, however, by a limit on sodium content of 200 milligrams per litre, which makes them low in sodium, like tap water.

Smoked foods
Smoked foods can contain up to 50 times more salt than the same, unsmoked foods. Fresh mackerel contains 0.15 g salt per 100 g, but smoked mackerel has 1.9 g salt per 100 g when smoked. Fresh salmon contains 0.1 g salt per 100 g, but smoked salmon has 4.7 g salt per 100 g. Luckily, we don't eat smoked salmon every day!

WAYS TO REDUCE YOUR SALT INTAKE

Here are 20 ways of avoiding hidden salt:

- Reduce the amount of salt used when cooking. Do this gradually and probably no one in the family will notice. Start with boiled vegetables first.
- If using canned vegetables, look for no added salt varieties.
- Rinse vegetables canned in brine through a sieve before heating up in ordinary water.
- Look for low salt or reduced salt alternatives of products like baked beans, ketchup, crisps (US potato chips), biscuits (cookies), butter, margarine, soups and gravy granules.
- Choose tinned fish, such as tuna, prepared in mineral water rather than brine.
- Read the labels and avoid monosodium glutamate.
- Offer low sodium salt at the table, unless you have kidney problems.
- Lessen the amount of salt added through stock cubes. I cut them in halves or quarters. Use the rest very soon, or throw it away. Better still, read below:
- Use herbs, garlic, spices, wine or lemon juice to add flavour.
- Avoid soy sauce, or use very occasionally.
- Avoid white bread, which tends to have more salt added. Choose reduced salt bread instead, or granary.
- Choose reduced salt breakfast cereal.
- Watch out for the bowls of salted nuts, olives and crisps at parties. There are unsalted varieties available, and at reasonable prices.
- Eat five portions of fruit and vegetables a day, unsalted of course.
- Eat bacon and sausages less frequently.
- Cut down on takeaways and ready meals. Avoid dehydrated pasta meals.
- Go for less salty cheeses, like ricotta, cottage, mozzarella and Swiss cheeses.
- Cut down on mayonnaise, which has a high salt content.
- Avoid processed foods for at least certain days of the week.
- Make your own soup; much tastier, cheap and less salty.

THE HEALTH BENEFITS OF SALT

Well, after all the doom and gloom of the problems associated with salt, it is good to know that some people get benefits from it, even though these are mostly topical.

SALT BATHS

After delivering my first child I was told to take a bath with a cup of salt dissolved in it. I thought that, since I was in a military hospital and the midwives were all unmarried and childless, this was one of their ways of getting back at you if you went over time in the delivery suite. (I did, by several hours.) Some of them also went for the dry shave before delivery, just to make it more uncomfortable as well. But, the salt bath is a great way of cleaning and preventing infection.

You can find a salt bath recipe in the rituals and customs section, if you fancy it.

SALT GARGLES FOR SORE THROAT

The age-old remedy for a sore throat is to gargle with a salt water solution. Since you don't swallow the salt (yuck!) it can be soothing and it allows salt to use its properties of cleaning and disinfecting. I remember several years ago being surprised when I visited our GP with a sore throat. I was expecting the usual antibiotics, but was sent packing with instructions to gargle twice a day for a few days instead. Half the time a sore throat will not be cured by antibiotics anyway.

MOUTH ULCERS

Gargling with salt water stings, but only in the same way that if you have a sore mouth you want to eat something salty to make it hurt, if you know what I mean. It does work!

THE DEAD SEA

The mineral content of the Dead Sea, combined with the lack of pollen and other allergens, has great benefits to some patients with respiratory problems. Reduced ultraviolet solar radiation and higher atmospheric pressure also benefit some people.

People suffering from cystic fibrosis apparently benefit from the atmosphere here, where oxygen levels are higher.

People suffering from skin disorders also benefit, in two different ways. Firstly, the reduction in harmful rays means that they can expose their skin to the sun for longer periods and secondly, the salts in the water have been shown to help psoriasis patients.

Year round sun, dry air and low levels of pollution all help.

Some popular therapies are:

- Climatotherapy and heliotherapy — that's your sunbathing, taking the air, etc.
- Thalassotherapy, or bathing in Dead Sea water.
- Balneotherapy, or treatment with black mineral mud.

Salt in Customs, Religions & Rituals

SALT IN CUSTOMS, RELIGIONS AND RITUALS

Salt has played an important role in many diverse religious and cultural customs for thousands of years. In both Islam and Judaism, salt is used to seal a bargain, because it is unchangeable. Even when it is dissolved it is still salt and can be returned to its original state. The ancient Egyptians, Greeks and Romans all included salt in sacrifices and offerings, and they called upon deities and gods using salt and water. It has been suggested that this may be the origin of Christian holy water.

Add to these ancient beliefs an array of other rituals and superstitions and you have a rich source of material. This section is intended to give a very brief summary of various beliefs, customs and rituals.

> *"Salt is born of the purest of parents:*
> *the sun and the sea."*
> PYTHAGORAS (580–500 BC)

ANCIENT CIVILIZATIONS
The Druids used salt in their rituals at Stonehenge. It is thought that this was as a symbol of the life-giving fruits of the earth. Salt is associated with life and health, and is used in rites of passage ceremonies in some cultures. It is also associated with good and has been used to counteract the effects of evil. Homer called salt divine and Plato termed it a 'substance dear to the Gods'. Since salt was so valuable — indeed, life depends on salt — it is hardly surprising that it found its way into the religious beliefs and practices of the worshippers.

Greek worshippers consecrated salt in their rituals and most ancient civilizations were accompanied by myths, religious and magic rites involving salt. The ancient Greeks and the Hebrews used salt during sacrifices.

GOOD TRIUMPHING OVER EVIL
The widespread notion that spilling salt will reap evil consequences is probably a relic of the sacred character of salt in early times. Anyone unfortunate enough to spill salt is supposed to incur the anger of all good spirits.

As a child I remember various older members of the family throwing salt over their shoulders (was it left or right?) if some was spilled. I also remember someone younger, pointing out that from a scientific point of view, salt would damage the floor covering. Another superstition I recall was not offering to dispense salt for anyone else, in the days when salt was always sprinkled on food, even before tasting it. Someone would invariably shout 'Help you to salt, help you to sorrow', if this happened. Perhaps the response should have been to throw some over the shoulder to recompense in some way. Still, worse things happen at sea (on the briny?).

HATCHES, MATCHES AND DISPATCHES

Similarities exist across continents and cultures. A range of traditions and rituals spans the human life cycle events of birth, marriage and death. Throughout the ages, there has been a belief in the sacred properties of salt.

BIRTH RITUALS
- The practice in Europe of protecting newborn babies, either by putting salt on their tongues or by submerging them in salt water, pre-dates Christian baptism. In Roman times a baby was rubbed with salt on the eighth day after birth, to keep away the demons and evil spirits. Until the practice was abolished in 1408 in France, children were salted until they were baptized.

- The Book of Ezekiel mentions rubbing newborn infants with salt to protect them from evil.

- In Holland, the practice was modified to placing salt in the cradle with the child.

- In the Catholic Church, salt has been used in a variety of purifying rituals, one of which was to place a small taste of salt on a baby's lip at the baptism with the words *accipe sal sapiente* ('receive enlightening salt'), meaning that wisdom should flavour man's entire life.

MARRIAGE

- In the Pyrenees, bridal couples went to church with salt in their left pockets to guard against impotence.

- In some parts of France, only one partner carried salt, either the groom or the bride. This is also the country that still conducts processions around the local area with the effigy of the groom on a gallows. Nice touch — what kind of taste does that leave in the mouth, I wonder?

- In Germany, in the past, the bride's shoes were sprinkled with salt.

- It is customary in some countries to greet newly-weds with gifts of salt and bread, instead of throwing confetti.

DEATH

- In the Buddhist tradition, salt repels evil spirits. Apparently, it is customary to throw salt over your shoulder before entering the house after a funeral, in order to scare off any evil spirits that may be clinging to your back.

- In 1933, the Dalai Lama was buried sitting up in a bed of salt. This was a common practice among some ancient groups of people. The dying person was encouraged to sit before death to make the process easier.

- In Wales there was a tradition of putting a plate of bread and salt on the coffin. A local professional sin-eater would arrive to eat the salt before burial of the deceased.

- A popular custom still in use in a number of countries requires that a handful of salt be thrown in the coffin of a dead person before the burial.

OTHER TRADITIONS

JAPANESE
- In Japan, where salt is obtained only from the sea, a salt culture has developed that can be traced in the rituals of everyday life, including meal preparation, sports and ceremony. Shinto religion uses salt to purify. Before sumo wrestlers enter the ring for a match, a handful of salt is thrown into the centre to drive off malevolent spirits.

- Before each performance in Japanese theatres, salt was sprinkled on to the stage to prevent evil spirits from casting spells and spoiling plays.

SCOTLAND
- In Scotland, salt was held in high repute as a charm. The salt box was the first object to be moved into a new dwelling. Robert Burns recalled in 1789 that on moving house he was escorted there by a procession of relatives carrying a bowl of salt.

- Also in Scotland, in ancient times, it was the tradition to add salt when brewing beer, to prevent ruination by witches and evil spirits. Mind you, adding salt to yeast prevents excess fermentation, so maybe there was more to it than superstition.

INDIA
- A gift of salt in India shows good wishes and recalls Gandhi's salt walk, which you can read about in the history section.

- Nagin women were sacred prostitutes known as 'wives of the snake god' in India. From time to time they would give up salt and go begging, giving half of the proceeds to priests for buying salt for the villagers.

- Indian troops pledged their loyalty to the British with salt.

GREECE

- In Greece salt is considered to have great powers as a purifying force. It can be used to ward off demons and evil spirits by being thrown over your left shoulder.

- A new house can be purified by sprinkling it with salt to remove any demons or lurking evil spirits.

- You can remove an unwanted guest or someone who has overstayed their welcome by sprinkling salt where the person will sit or by throwing it behind them. This is not as effective if the person sees you. It'll probably have the desired effect though, if they think you've gone potty!

- Salt should be covered up at night because if the moon or stars see the salt the carrier of the salt will develop warts or a rash. So if you are eating an open bag of chips in Greece, watch out!

GOOD OR BAD LUCK?

- Hamburg, in Germany, renews its good luck every year by parading a bread loaf covered in chocolate and a marzipan salt cellar filled with bread through the streets. This presumably recalls the great wealth brought from the salt trade in the Middle Ages and the famous Lübeck marzipan as well.

- In the past, Germans took oaths of allegiance with their hand sunk in it.

- In medieval times, salt was never touched at the table by hands but only with the point of a knife for the sake of purity and manners.

- Sailors in days gone by would not mention salt while at sea. Salt was never thrown overboard.

- Anglo-Saxon farmers included salt in the magic ingredients placed in a hole in the plough, as they ensured good harvests.

- In Borneo, when tribesmen returned from killing, they gave up salt and sex for a period of time. This also happened among some Native American tribes.

- Salt in Arab countries was used to seal a bargain and as a sign of friendship. It also served as a sort of insurance: if you ate another man's salt in his house you could not harm him and he could not hurt you.

- The Hopi people had a legend that angry warrior twins punished mankind by placing salt deposits far away from civilization, just to make it hard and dangerous to harvest the precious mineral.

- A 16th-century book of Jewish Law explains the only safe way of handling salt: with the middle two fingers. If the thumb was used, a man's children would die; use of the little finger would bring poverty and use of his index finger may make him become a murderer. No good throwing a pinch over your shoulder there, then.

- Bringing bread and salt to a new home is a Jewish tradition dating back to the Middle Ages.

- Salt is believed to be able to drive off demons. Apparently, you won't find salt served at a witches' sabbath or in any pagan religious offering. This also applies to some African and Caribbean ceremonies, where spirits are summoned and the salt might keep them away.

- In Haiti it is said that the only way to break a spell and bring a zombie back to life is with salt.

- In parts of Africa and the Caribbean, many people believed that evil spirits were disguised as women who shed their skin at night. They travelled in the dark as balls of fire. To destroy these spirits their skin had to be found and salted, so that they could not return to it in the morning.

- In Cervia, in Italy, the rite of the Virgin of the Fire dates from the 18th century. In February, a parade of salt workers carry a huge crucifix, rejected by the sea, to Forli. The mystery of how it got there gave rise to its use as a symbol of protection for the workers against illness and disaster, as well as for a good salt harvest. Locals believe that if you keep Cervian salt in your house, you and your family will live a long and healthy life.

- You should never pass salt directly to someone. Always put the salt cellar down on the table, otherwise it means passing on sorrow. This can also be averted by passing the salt and pepper together. It's also, apparently, good etiquette to pass both together.

ROMAN RELIGION AND SALT

Roman religion and mythology, although based on the Greek model, underwent several changes and other influences, making it a more complex mix of traditions, with separate cults as well.

SACRIFICIAL LAMBS

During Roman times, sacrifices of animals were used to please various gods. Sacrificial millstones were prepared by first rubbing them with salt. Domestic sacrifices were practised for different occasions and were often followed by a banquet in which most of the sacrifice was eaten. The first act of *Ritus Romanus* was the consecration of the victim, where the sacrificer, usually the head of the household, consecrated the victim by the *mola salsa*. This was roasted wheat flour with added salt, associated with the fire of Vesta, goddess of the hearth. In order to do this, the sacrificer powdered the back of the animal with the *mola salsa* and poured a little wine on its forehead. Some say that if the salt fell from the head of the sacrifice's chosen victim, it was a sign of bad luck.

Salt made other appearances during sacrifice in the form of offerings. *Penates*, the household gods, protected the household's food supply, and were worshipped or appeased so that the family would not go hungry or be unable to offer hospitality. Most families would keep a salt cellar and first fruits of the season on the family dining table for the *Penates*.

For general offerings to the *Penates*, wine and cakes were used. A two-month-old piglet might be offered, but it wasn't considered a good omen to make such an offering on your birthday. Fair enough: I think sharing a cake with your family and friends is a much nicer idea.

For funerals, when a ewe, pig or lamb would be slaughtered, boiled salted wheat was offered. For offerings to *Manes*, in honour of deceased loved ones, milk, wine and salted corn were added, along with the blood of a ewe, pig or bull calf. *Ceres*, goddess of crops and harvests (from whom we have the word 'cereal'), was honoured with bread, salt, incense and the first harvest goods.

During the second and third centuries AD, the worship of the Iranian god of the sun, justice, war and contract grew into a cult among Roman soldiers. The god was called *Mithra* by the Romans, and its following took the form of a secret cult, very Dan Brown style, complete with initiation ceremonies and seven levels of enlightenment. *Mithraism* was the way in which subjects honoured this deity by loyalty to the emperor. Worship involved the sacrifice of a bull in one of many underground caves in which a well or spring was present. The soldiers possibly used some of their *salarium* or payment to acquire the salted meat consumed.

The Roman goddess of health, safety and welfare, called *Salus*, was identified with the Greek *Hygieia*, presumably where we get the word hygiene from. Her temple was the scene of an annual sacrifice, in August.

Februa were purifying elements or instruments which the Romans believed averted evils resulting from contact with forbidden objects. Salt was used as a talisman here, along with water, fire, wool and laurel. Evils, whether physical or spiritual, could be washed or burned away by the use of these objects.

MUMMIFICATION AND PRESERVATION

EGYPTIAN MUMMIFICATION
The earliest Egyptian mummies date back to around 3200 BC. The process of mummification was described by the Greek historian, Herodotus. This involved laying the body in a bath of natron, the sodium mineral used by the Egyptians for brining, for at least 70 days. Sodium salt solution has a desiccating effect of attracting water from the tissues, since the salt solution water pressure is considerably lower than the tissue liquids. For mummification to occur, all water must be removed from the body and there must be little or no decomposition from bacterial action. Understandably, most mummies have been discovered in desert environments, although remains discovered in acidic peat bogs and glacial regions have also been preserved.

The process developed refinements over the years, but initially the body was treated with natron and then wrapped in bandages that had been soaked in a sort of resin.

Later, by around 1500 BC, morticians would first remove the brain and vital organs and pack the cavities with natron, sawdust or sand and immerse the body for about six weeks. After this time, the body was washed, treated with spices and more natron and wrapped in bandages for a further 30 days or so. These remains have given scientists and archaeologists plenty of information about diet and health of the time. The many artefacts discovered buried with the mummies included food, tools, clothing and jewellery. Sometimes pets were buried with their masters.

SACRIFICE AND PRESERVATION

The process for preserving meat from slaughtered animals by dehydration was similar to that used for burials. The result was to dehydrate the meat to a point where no bacteria could grow and cause decomposition. This method has been found in many cultures and religions.

Following the animal slaughter the carcass was drained of blood by slinging the animal up in a hanging position and letting gravity do most of the rest. The last of the blood and body fluids was drawn off by dehydrating the carcass. This was achieved by soaking in brine or by placing it in a bed of salt crystals. Other methods involved broiling with vinegar or using oils and spices.

The process of dehydration was well known to most ancient civilizations, and was the most efficient method of preserving meat when salt was easily available, although the method was not used by all communities.

FROM ABATTOIR TO TEMPLE
Preparing the concentrated brine needed an advanced water and drainage system. One such example was the hydraulic system in the Temple of Solomon in Jerusalem, or the First Temple, utilizing freshwater springs and a reservoir. The water was directed through the Temple by gravity, where baths were available for salting meat.

The Temple was a religious focal point and the ritual of sacrifice and salting became part of a covenant for the Jewish religion. It was completed in the 10th century BC by Solomon, the son of King David, but destroyed in 586 BC by the Babylonians. The concentration of religious ritual at the Temple made Jerusalem a place of pilgrimage and an important commercial centre.

SOLOMON'S TEMPLE
A laver was the sacred wash-bowl of the tabernacle and a basin for the water used by the priests in their ablutions. The one originally used in the tabernacle was of brass. The inner court of the priests contained the altar of burnt offering, the Brazen Sea and ten lavers used for sacrifice. The lavers, each of which held the equivalent of 40 baths, rested on portable holders made of bronze, provided with wheels and ornamented with figures of lions and palm trees.

The Brazen or Molten Sea was a laver measuring an impressive 5 m (16 ft) wide, 2.5 m (8 ft) deep and with a circumference of 15 m (49 ft), resting on the backs of 12 oxen. The capacity is said to have been 2,000 baths, or 80,000 litres (21,133 gallons). The priests used this laver when they washed their hands and feet on entering the tabernacle. It stood in the court between the altar and the door.

Many other religions and traditions developed as a result. People worshipping at temples also used baths for washing hands and feet before entering. The design is said to have been based on an area the Babylonians used in their temple rituals. Such a pity they had to destroy the original!

The reconstructed temple in Jerusalem, which stood between 516 BC and AD 70, was the Second Temple, rebuilt and expanded by King Herod. This reworking sat nicely with his harbour at Caesarea, inaugurated in 9 BC. His monopoly of the salt supply from the Dead Sea mountain provided the Temple with a highly profitable source of income. The port was the ideal way of exporting the salt to Rome, which was having trouble with supplies by then due to rises in sea level. This was at a time when salt supplies were unavailable from the Mediterranean because of flooding.

JEWISH FOOD LAWS

The word kosher or *kashrut*, is translated as 'fitting' or 'correct'. Kosher or koshering salt is a form of salt that has irregularly shaped crystals. The crystals make it suitable for preparing meat in accordance with *kashrut* law because the increased surface area of the crystals absorbs blood more effectively. Kosher laws ensured the hygienic processing of meat by dehydration. All liquids had to be removed. The requirement in ancient times is carried on today, and aims to prevent the meat from deteriorating. In this way it can be consumed long after the animal has been slaughtered. Given that butter needs a 2 per cent salt solution, meat 6 per cent and fish 20 per cent, this could lead to up to 100 grams of salt being consumed per day. This law for preparing meat is a theme in many other religions.

Kosher slaughter requires all animals and birds to be slaughtered by a trained person using a special method. Blood must be thoroughly removed from all meat, using one of several methods such as soaking and salting, or broiling. Any utensils, or whole kitchens, which are used with non-kosher foods, are generally considered to make otherwise kosher food non-kosher.

STAR OF DAVID

During times when Jewish slaves were held by Egyptians along the Nile, they made salt briquettes from straw left in brine. Like the formations made today for tourism and artefacts (see Fascinating Facts chapter), strong geometric shapes such as crosses, squares and stars (formed from two equilateral triangles) were used and planted vertically in the brine pans to allow crystallization to occur. It has been suggested that the Star of David as a symbol of Judaism may have evolved from these straw stars.

As described above, Jewish Temple offerings included salt. On Friday evenings, the start of the Jewish Sabbath, Jews still dip their bread in salt as a remembrance of those sacrifices. Bread is the symbol of food and salt preserves this food.

BIBLE REFERENCES

Covenants in both the Old and New Testaments were sealed with salt. Hebrew salt was the symbol of the eternal nature of God's covenant with Israel. In the Book of Numbers, it says, 'It is a covenant of salt forever, before the Lord', and in Chronicles, 'The Lord God of Israel gave the kingdom over Israel to David forever, even to him, and to his sons, by a covenant of salt.'

The importance of salt in ancient times is apparent through the numerous references to it in the Bible. For example, the Book of Job, in the Old Testament, raises the question: 'Can nothing which is unsavoury be eaten without salt?'

The most well-known reference is probably that which tells of Lot's wife. Lot, a nephew of Abraham, lived with his wife and two daughters in Sodom. Just before the city was destroyed for its acts of sin, two angels came to Lot and warned him to escape. They told him and his family not to look back once they had left. Lot's wife, however, couldn't resist turning to look back at the burning city and as punishment she was turned into a pillar of salt.

It is thought that the colour of brine, which can take on a red appearance in some circumstances, was responsible for the Moabites' interpretation of water 'as red as blood'. Red brine not only looks like blood but also tastes like it and leaves a deep and disturbing impression. It has been suggested that the red salt pans at Sodom, at the southern end of the Dead Sea, may be derived from the Hebrew words for field and red.

When Elisha sweetened the waters of Jericho, he cast salt into them to illustrate its purifying power. Since the earliest times salt has been associated with value and worthiness. The Bible reference, 'Witness, we are the salt of the earth,' is also echoed by Jesus who called his disciples the 'salt of the earth'. This is said to show them as men who were able to keep others from corruption and sin.

A primary source of salt was the shore of the Dead Sea or the Salt Sea as it is called many times in the Bible. Jesus is said to have told his followers: 'You are the salt of the earth, but if the salt has lost its taste, it is good for nothing except to be thrown out and trodden under the foot of men.'

In the New Testament salt is represented in a great number of metaphors or in parables as a symbol of wisdom, incorruptibility, eternity and alliance between God and man. This may account for Leonardo da Vinci's depiction in *The Last Supper* of Judas Iscariot with an upturned salt cellar in front of him. This symbol is thought to represent the covenant of friendship and love broken by Judas in his betrayal of Jesus.

A HINDU STORY

Hinduism is not one religion but a family of religions. It is a whole complex of beliefs and institutions that have appeared from the time of the ancient and most sacred scriptures.

The Upanishads, composed during the period 800 to 600 BC, convey the idea of secret teaching. The following story teaches about the commonality of divine essence: the self of the whole world, Brahman.

A father told his son to put a piece of salt in a container of water and come back the next day. The son did as he was told. The next day the father told the son to bring him the piece of salt. He groped for it but could not find it, as it had dissolved completely.

"Take a sip from this corner," said the father, "how does it taste?"
"Salty," was the reply.
"Take a sip from the centre — how does it taste?"
"Salty."
"Take a sip from that corner — how does it taste?"
"Salty."
"Look for the salt again," said the father.
The son said, "I cannot see the salt. I only see water."
The father told him, "You, of course, did not see it there, yet it was always right there. In the same way, you cannot see the spirit, but in truth he is there."

An invisible and subtle essence is the spirit of the whole universe. It is the essence of Hinduism that there are many different ways of looking at a single object, none of which will give the whole view, but each of which is entirely valid in its own right.

OTHER BELIEFS

The fact that salt is a natural preservative and antiseptic means it has long been used as a purifying agent in folk magic and traditions. Many Wiccan traditions recommend ritual bathing before any major spell can work. Ritual bathing allows participants to wash away the mundane world, as they prepare for the spiritual. By taking a ritual bath and using the items saved only for magical purposes, many people believe they begin to put themselves in a spiritual mindset. On occasions when participants must travel to the ritual site after the bath has been taken, they may need to refresh themselves by taking a spray bottle full of pure water and a tablespoon or two of special ritual salts or some sea salt and sage. This spritz is said to refresh you and revitalize the feelings of the ritual bath, making it easier for you to get into a spiritual frame of mind.

Salt has a long history of use in rituals of purification, magical protection and blessing. Among spell-casters working in the European tradition, it is commonplace to lay down a pinch of salt in each corner of a room before performing a spell. This has carried over into contemporary African-American voodoo practice as well.

When the intention of a spell is protective, salt may be used alone or combined with ingredients like saltpetre and black pepper. For more aggressive spells against enemies, salt may be added to red pepper, sulphur and bluestone. Ritual cleaning is an important facet of African folk magic and salt is a common ingredient in protection spells.

Cooking
with Salt

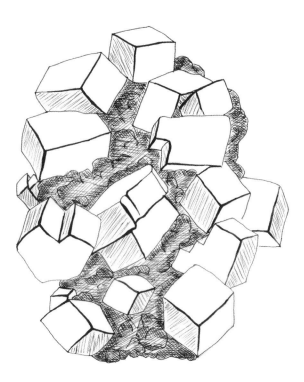

COOKING WITH SALT

The normal procedure for this series of books would require this section to be all about using the foodstuff in many recipes over as wide a range of dishes and courses as possible. Salt is the exception because it mustn't be eaten in vast quantities. After putting the case for eating less salt it would be contradictory, to say the least. There are, however, some dishes that need salt to taste right and complete an important part of the process, such as bread-making and other procedures outlined below. Some, such as porridge-making, may appear to need salt, too, although, not being a Scot, I find I can eat porridge without it.

Because we shouldn't eat too much salt it doesn't mean that we can't indulge on occasions, or use salt to prepare a dish. The methods described here, therefore, are included because this is a book about the uses of salt. The recipes have been chosen because they need salt in the preparation, or because they are so bizarre, interesting or unusual, I just had to share them. As always, I leave it to you to decide what to do with them.

THE USES OF SALT IN COOKING

THERMAL PROPERTIES, HOT AND COLD

You may have been surprised to read in an earlier section that salt is used in ice cream making. This is not only for flavouring, but also to use its thermal properties. Rock salt dissolving in ice water pulls heat from its surroundings. Ice cream makers sit the salt-and-ice mixture in an insulated container, and inside that is placed a highly conductive container of the cream mixture, which freezes rapidly.

Salt can be used to cook food as well. Large amounts of rock salt are heated in an oven to temperatures around 200°C (400°F). Once the salt gets hot, the food is placed in the salt and another layer of preheated salt is poured on top. This method is an extremely fast way to get heat into food and means cooking times can be shortened. You can follow some recipes for this style of cooking later in this chapter.

Adding salt to boiling water apparently raises the temperature very slightly as well as flavouring the food. The amount of salt should vary according to the amount of water and quite a lot is usually used. On reflection, I think I'll stick to not salting the potatoes or pasta and cook them for a minute longer.

REMOVING BITTERNESS

Some foods respond well to salting before cooking, to remove liquid or bitterness and to alter the texture, such as the aubergine. Another technique is to sweat onions or garlic over a low heat to draw out their moisture and soften them.

ENHANCING SWEETNESS

Salt also tends to enhance our perception of other flavours, particularly that of sweetness. This explains its use in ice cream, for example, or kettle corn. Most confectionery recipes have a small amount of salt which, though it cannot be directly detected, has a noticeable effect on the final result.

BINDING AND TEXTURIZING AGENT

Salt acts as a binder, as it helps to extract the proteins in processed and formed meats, binding the meat together and reducing cooking losses. It strengthens gluten in bread dough, providing uniform grain, texture and strength. Salt allows the dough to expand without tearing. It also helps to harden rind and develop an even consistency in cheese.

COLOURING

Salt gives processed meats, such as ham, bacon and hot dogs, more colour when used with sugar and nitrate. It also enhances the golden colour in bread crust by increasing the caramelization process.

FERMENTATION CONTROL

In baked products such as bread and some cakes, salt controls fermentation by retarding the growth of bacteria, yeast and moulds. It has also been used in brewing to prevent excess fermentation.

PRESERVATION AND PROCESSING
Salting is one of the oldest food preservation methods.
Before refrigeration and freezing it was about the only
method used in the home. Even since the development of
refrigeration, salt preserving has remained an important
aid to food hygiene. Sodium chloride helps prevent
spoiling, by drawing water out of the food and depriving
bacteria of the moisture needed for them to thrive. As
an antibacterial agent, salt performs well at killing some
of the bacteria that would cause spoiling. Today there
are many other methods used commercially, including
pasteurization, dehydration and freeze-drying, irradiation
and the use of chemical preservatives, as described
earlier. Each of the newer processes is good news in
terms of the reduction of salt intake as an ingredient.

Some cultural traditions use a lot more salt than others,
so preparing food in the oriental or Indian style will
suggest more salt or the inclusion of salty sauces, such as
soy sauce. If you prepare your own food you have the
choice of leaving a lot (or all) of the salt out. It doesn't
help though if you prepare all your stir-fry ingredients
and then buy a jar of sauce which is highly salted.

Other foods such as smoked meat or fish have more salt
than you might think. Some are very high in salt, so
eating them less often would be a sensible option

SMOKED AND CURED MEAT

The smoking process includes adding salt to preserve the
meat, fish or other food. Prepared food is salted or
soaked in brine and placed in an oven and smoked for
up to two days. Unsmoked bacon will also be high in salt,
as it has been prepared with salt.

PORK BELLY TO BACON
I have never tried this myself, so include it for those who
might be interested in reading about the theory of how
to produce home-made bacon.

Choice of meat
Use the belly meat closest to the loin, the meatiest part of the belly. Begin with fresh bellies that have been properly chilled. If you are using a whole side of belly pork, cut it into three pieces for ease of handling.

BRINED OR WET-CURED BACON
This is a much milder form of curing, and the meat is cured in the brine under refrigeration. As meat keeps fresh longer at lower temperatures, it does not require so much salt.

The ingredients of brine for curing are salt and sugar. The sugar helps to keep the meat moist and soft as it ages and takes away some of the harshness of the salt. The salt in the brine is used to pull moisture out of the meat and preserve it from bacteria. Brining also prepares the meat for smoking, which brings a lot of flavour, aroma and perhaps colour to the bacon, depending on what you use. Nitrates and nitrites are often included as antibacterial agents and to ensure a pink hue on the meat, but they don't have to be used. Commercially prepared brines are available, but not necessary. If you are going to all the trouble of making your own bacon, why use a commercial product? Make enough brine to fill a non-metallic container that allows you to completely submerse your pork bellies.

BRINE RECIPES

You will need for Brine I:
For each 2 litres (3$\frac{1}{4}$ pints) of chilled water, add
300 g (10$\frac{1}{2}$ oz) pickling salt
100 g (3$\frac{1}{2}$ oz) soft brown sugar

You will need (optional):

2 tsp black pepper	12 allspice berries
4 bay leaves	2 cinnamon sticks
4 garlic cloves	1 giant shallot
12 juniper berries	Sprigs of sage

You will need for Brine II:
>   For each 3.6 litres (1 gallon) of water, add
>   750 g (about 1$\frac{1}{2}$ lb) salt
>   1 kg (2$\frac{1}{5}$ lb) brown sugar

Method:
1. Heat up the brine in a pot, steep it with fresh herb sprigs, shallots, garlic, juniper berries, etc., until the solids have dissolved.
2. Cool it down, strain and cool it again.
3. Submerge the belly pork and let it sit for two to four days, depending on the size of the belly.

Curing method
This assumes you have a BIG refrigerator which should be between 2°C and 4°C (about 38°F).

Place the container with the submerged pork bellies in a refrigerator for four days. Use plates to weigh down the bellies if they float to the top. Turn the meat.

Preparation for smoking
1. Rinse the pork bellies with fresh water, and dry thoroughly. Before smoking the bellies, they must be left to dry further so that a pellicle forms on the outside of the meat. This forms as a result of water-soluble proteins being brought to the surface. When dry, these proteins form a sticky coating over the meat, which will absorb the smoke much better. The meat won't take smoke anyway until the surface is dry. If the meat is smoked when still damp, it will be inferior in taste and colour.
2. Elevate the meat on cooling racks and set up a fan to blow over it for about 30 minutes each side and speed up the drying process. Turn the meat over halfway through. The meat takes on a surface sheen when the pellicle has formed.

Source of wood for smoke
Only hardwood sawdust or chips should be used for smoking. Don't use pine. Apple and cherry woods both give a mild, slightly sweet, fruity smoke. Hickory and oak give a strong, more robust flavour.

Maple gives sweet smoke: good for bacon with pancakes.

Cold smoking
This ensures smoking and penetration over a low temperature for a long period.

Method:
1. Hang the pork bellies on bacon hangers in a smoker.
2. Try to keep the temperature of the smoker between 27–38°C (80–100°F). Smoke the meat for about 8 hours.

DRY-CURED BACON

This is the oldest method. From Saxon times pigs were fattened on acorns (mast) in the autumn before slaughtering in November. The meat would keep the family going through the winter. Each farmhouse would have its own recipe and a slab of bacon would be kept above the fireplace. Heavily salted bacon would be part of the rations for long sea journeys and would make it very tough and dry.

This recipe produces a salty, streaky bacon. It can be added to stews, soups and sauces. The amount of dry cure may vary, but the proportions should be as follows:

You will need for Dry Cure I:
750 g (about 1$\frac{1}{2}$ lb) salt
250 g (9 oz) soft brown sugar
25 g (1 oz) freshly ground black pepper

You will need (optional):
Bay leaves
20 juniper berries, lightly crushed
25 g (1 oz) coriander seeds, crushed

You will need for Dry Cure II:
Use in the following proportions:
50 g (2 oz) salt
60 g (3 oz) brown sugar
40 g (1$\frac{1}{2}$ oz) ground peppercorns

Method:

1. Mix the salt, sugar and pepper in a non-metallic bowl. Add any optional spices.

2. Take one piece of belly at a time and prepare on a clean surface by rubbing all over with the dry cure mix.

3. Place in a clean, non-metallic tray (plastic is ideal), and repeat with the other pieces.

4. Pile the pieces on top of each other and leave, covered, in a cool place for 24 hours. Use a cover to keep any flies away if this is not a refrigerator. Keep any leftover cure. When the meat has leached the liquid, drain this off and use the rest of the salt to rub over the meat. Restack the meat with the top piece in the middle and the bottom piece on top.

5. Continue for at least four days, reordering the pile each day. You can leave the pork for up to ten days.

6. Rinse off the salt, dry off the meat and wrap in clean muslin. Hang in a well-ventilated place and use as required by cutting off slices or chunks and rewrapping. If you are not going to use all of the meat within a month, consider freezing some of it.

Meat that has been salted for long periods will be very salty, so you may need to soak in clean water for some time to reduce the salinity, in the same way that ham needs to be soaked before boiling or roasting.

HOME-CURED BACON WITH LENTILS

Here is a recipe to celebrate the use of your home-cured bacon. If very salty, soak it first for an hour or so in cold water.

You will need: Serves 4

    4 thick slices home cured bacon with the rind on
    1 onion
    2 carrots
    2 celery sticks
    1 bayleaf
    4 tbsp lentils

Method:

1. Chop the vegetables roughly and put in a pan with the pork.
2. Bring to the boil, and simmer very gently for 1¹/₂ hours, until tender.
3. Remove the vetetables with a slotted spoon and put in the lentils. Simmer for about 20 minutes.
4. Serve bacon on a bed of lentils and pour over a little of the liquid from the pan.

MILD BRINE FOR CURING MEAT

This is a simple, quick, all-purpose mild brine for beef, chicken, turkey and pork. It can be used when grilling chicken pieces and the meat will never be dry.

> For 1 litre (2 pints) water add
> 60 g (2 oz) salt
> 30 g (1 oz) sugar

1. Mix cold water, salt and sugar and stir to dissolve.
2. In a non-metallic container, immerse food (not frozen) in brine, seal and refrigerate for an hour per 500 g (1 lb) of meat. Don't leave for more than 8 hours.

SPICED AND SALTED BEEF

This takes a lot of planning ahead, but the result is truly delicious: a real Christmas special.

You will need: Serves 12

> 3 kg (7 lb) beef brisket, on the bone
> 175 g (6 oz) coarse salt
> 4 tbsp soft brown sugar
> 1 tbsp black peppercorns, crushed
> 1 tbsp ground allspice
> 6 juniper berries, crushed (optional)
> 1 tsp saltpetre
> 1 tsp ground mace
> 1 tsp ground cloves
> 1 tsp fresh nutmeg, grated

Method:

1. Place the beef in a ceramic or plastic bowl. Rub the salt well into the beef, cover and refrigerate for 12 to 24 hours.
2. Remove the meat, drain the liquid off and return the beef to the bowl.
3. Mix all of the other ingredients together and rub into the meat, ensuring good coverage. Cover with foil or cling film and return to the refrigerator for 10–12 days, turning the meat daily and basting with the juices that collect.
4. To cook, put the meat and juices in a large pan and cover with cold water. Bring to the boil and then simmer for 3–3½ hours. Leave to cool in the pan for another hour.
5. When cool enough, remove the bone and press the meat between two plates with a weight on top. Chill overnight before slicing.

CORNED BEEF

This name for preserved beef dates from the 1600s. The word 'corn' comes from an Anglo-Saxon word for granule and refers to the grains of salt used to make the brine in which the beef soaked. When Europeans went to the Americas, the term corn stuck as the name for any grain. In the New World, the most common grain was the maize the natives grew and what we now call maize. Corned beef is really salted beef, but modern refrigeration has meant that milder brines have been used to create what we know as corned beef.

BOILED SALT BEEF WITH DUMPLINGS

You can buy your beef already salted and cook at home.

You will need: Serves 6

  1.5 kg (3½ lb) salted silverside or brisket beef
  2 large onions, whole
  6 cloves, stuck into the onions
  ½ tsp ground mace
  ½ tsp grated nutmeg
  12 crushed black peppercorns

You will need for the dumplings:
    110 g (4 oz) self-raising (self-rising) flour
    55 g (2 oz) suet (chilled, grated shortening)
    Salt and black pepper
    2 tbsp chopped parsley
    1 tbsp horseradish sauce

Method:
1. Put the beef into a pan with the onions and cloves. Add the spices and pepper and just cover with cold water.
2. Bring to the boil then simmer gently for 3$\frac{1}{2}$ hours, uncovered.
3. Remove the meat to a serving dish and keep warm. Keep half of the liquid in the pan and reduce to thicken the rest in another saucepan while you make the dumplings.
4. Sieve flour and add the suet, herbs and seasoning. Add the horseradish and a little water to make a sticky dough that will gather in a ball. Lightly flour your hands and make small dumplings.
5. Poach the dumplings in the remaining liquid from the meat until just cooked. Serve the beef and dumplings hot with mashed potatoes and carrots.

SMOKED AND CURED FISH

Smoking has been used as a means of preserving fish for a long time. Carp, buffalo catfish, salmon, trout and chubs may be successfully smoked. Certain steps in the process require careful attention. As with brined and smoked bacon, there are four steps to smoking fish:

- Brining or salting
- Curing
- Drying to form a pellicle
- Smoking

You can read about some other forms of smoked and preserved fish in the chapter on fascinating facts.

Brining
To tell if you have used enough salt, float an egg in the mixture. As long as the egg floats you have enough salt (about 80 per cent).

SMOKED SALMON

You will need:
  22—44 kg (10—20 lb) salmon fillets
  1.5 kg ($3^1/_2$ lb) brown sugar
  3 kg (7 lb) salt
  22 litres (5 gallons) water

Method:
1. Cut fillets into even-sized pieces. Mix the salt, sugar and water. Mix enough brine to completely immerse the fish in the solution.
2. Cover the fish in brine and place the container(s) in a refrigerator for two hours
3. Remove fish from the brine and rinse under cold running water.
4. Place brined portions on to a greased smoking rack. Keep adequate space around each piece to allow the smoke to filter around the fish from all sides. Place racked fish into refrigeration for a minimum of 12 hours to allow the fish to cure and form a pellicle.
5. To smoke, start out as cool as possible and gradually increase temperature to 65°C (150°F) for 30 minutes. Remove rack from smoker and allow product to cool
6. The fish is now ready to be vacuum sealed or consumed. If vacuum sealed it must be kept refrigerated until you are ready to use it.

Now I know why I buy small packets of smoked salmon from a supermarket. It's much cheaper to buy in France, where we normally eat it, than in England.

GRAVADLAX

This is a traditional Swedish method of curing fish. Don't be tempted to add more alcohol, as the fish might go rubbery. Use within one week of preparation.

You will need:

 125 g (4^1/$_2$ oz) coarse sea salt
 150 g (5 oz) cup chopped fresh dill
 3 tbsp fresh grated orange zest
 1 tbsp fresh coarse ground black pepper
 80 ml (3 fl oz) vodka
 125 g (4^1/$_2$ oz) sugar
 1.4 kg (3 lb) tuna steaks, salmon or other fish fillets
     or steaks

Method:

1. If using fillets, leave the skin on and wrap in pairs with the skin side out. Wrap steaks individually.
2. In a non-metallic mixing bowl, combine all the ingredients except the fish.
3. Lay out several large pieces of plastic wrap. Rub the fish all over with the curing mix and cover with another plastic sheet.
4. Wrap tightly in several layers of plastic, packing the mix into the fish. Place this packet on a deep plate or baking dish and cover with another plate to weigh the fish down. The plastic will leak liquid, so be prepared. Add more weights on top and refrigerate for between one and four days to infuse.
5. When completed, unwrap, rinse in cold water to remove all of the cure. Pat dry and slice thinly with a sharp knife.

TRADITIONAL ALASKAN SALMON

This is a traditional way to preserve or dry salmon for the winter. The native people of Alaska still dry salmon on large wooden racks for use during the winter. This process remains in the realms of theory for me and is for interest only.

Method:

1. Slice the fillets lengthwise into 1.27 cm ($\frac{1}{2}$ in) wide strips. You can freeze them first to make cutting easier.
2. Make your brine.
3. Brine the strips for 10 minutes and then rinse under a cold tap.
4. Spray a rack with cooking oil. Hang the strips on the rack or tie strings from the strips to hang in the smokehouse.
5. Smoke at 27°C (80°F) for 24 hours. The strips should be dry to the touch but raw in the middle.
6. Remove for drying with a strong fan for two days or so.
7. Freeze the salmon. This will kill any parasites and prevent over-drying.

ITALIAN SARDINE FILLETS IN SALT

Method:

1. Cut off the head and take the innards out of the sardines.
2. Put the fillets on a plate in layers and cover each layer generously with salt.
3. After two hours, rub the salt from the fish and add some olive oil.
4. Grill until cooked.

SOUSED HERRINGS I

This is an easy recipe and can be used for mackerel as well.

You will need: Serves 4

    2 herrings per person
    2 bay leaves
    1 large sliced onion
    1 tsp pickling spice
    Malt vinegar and water to cover
    2 tbsp salt
    Pepper

Method:
1. Preheat the oven to 170°C (325°F, gas mark 3).
2. Clean the fish and remove the heads and tails. You don't need to fillet them.
3. Rub salt into the skin and lay them in an ovenproof dish. Add the bay leaves, pickling spice, onion and pepper.
4. Just cover the fish with a mixture of vinegar and water. Cover with foil or a lid and bake for 30 to 40 minutes.
5. Serve hot or cold, with a little of the liquid poured over.

SOUSED HERRINGS II

This is a faster recipe which doesn't need an oven, just a hot plate.

You will need: **Serves 2**
    6 fresh herring fillets
    1 tbsp salt
    1 tsp ground pepper
    Pinch of allspice
    2 small onions, finely chopped
    50 g (1$^1/_2$ oz) white sugar
    3 bay leaves
    2 tbsp water
    275 ml (10 fl oz) white wine vinegar

Method:
1. Sprinkle the fillets with salt, pepper and allspice. Add the onions and roll up the fillets, securing each with a toothpick.
2. Put the fish into a saucepan with the rest of the ingredients. Bring to the boil and simmer for 3—4 minutes.
3. Allow to cool in the pan. Serve cold.

COOKING IN SALT CRUSTS

This method of cooking uses salt to keep food moist and to seal in flavour. The instructions may look a little unorthodox, and the method is certainly not one you can use to knock up a quick meal.

CHICKEN IN A SALT CRUST WITH HAY

This dish has a lot of preparation, starting with a visit to the pet shop, unless you live on a farm or keep horses. You need a carrier bag of hay, not straw, to start with. Your own chickens would be advisable too, for the eggs.

You will need: **Serves 4**

1 medium-sized chicken   Black pepper
1 lemon   Bunch of thyme

You will need for the salt crust pastry:

50 g (2 oz) thyme, chopped   700 g (1 lb 7 oz) salt
50 g (2 oz) rosemary, chopped   12 egg whites
1.6 kg (3$^{1}/_{2}$ lb) strong plain   370 g (13 oz) water
   (all-purpose) flour

Method:
1. Soak the hay overnight and squeeze to dry.
2. Mix all the dry ingredients for the pastry together with the egg whites and herbs. Use enough water to form a dough which is not too wet.
3. Knead for 10 minutes, then cover and leave to rest in the refrigerator for a couple of hours. (You'll probably need a rest too by now!)
4. Preheat the oven to 220°C (425°F, gas mark 7).
5. Roll out the dough on to a floured surface to about 25 cm (10 in) in diameter. Put a portion of damp hay in the centre.
6. Season the chicken inside and out with pepper and stuff the lemon and the thyme inside. Put it upside down on the hay and cover with more hay. Wrap the dough around the bird to seal it in, making sure there are no holes in the pastry to let steam out.
7. Put the whole thing in a large ovenproof dish and cook for about 40 minutes. The pastry should be brown and dry.

8. Remove the chicken from the oven and leave it untouched for another 40 minutes. Carefully open the crust, keeping out of the way of hot steam escaping. Throw away the pastry and the hay.

9. Check that the chicken is thoroughly cooked before serving.

SALT-ENCRUSTED WHOLE FISH

As for the chicken recipe, the purpose of the salt is to cook the fish evenly without it drying out. The result is a very moist fish. Bass works well, but you can use any whole fish. You need to use sea salt, kosher salt or very coarse salt to prevent the fish from absorbing the salt. The amount of salt will vary, depending on the type and the size of the fish, but you will need at least as much salt as weight of fish.

You will need: **Serves 2**

> 1 whole bass, about 700 g (1$^1/_2$ lb), gutted and
>   scaled but not skinned
> 1 bunch of mixed herbs
> 1 sliced lemon

Method:

1. Preheat the oven to 240°C (475°F, gas mark 9) and line a baking tray with foil.

2. Rinse the fish in cold water and dry. Stuff with lemon slices and herbs. The herbs should keep the salt out of the fish, so be generous.

3. Pour salt to make a thick layer over the middle third of the lined pan. Place the fish on top. Pour more salt on top of the fish, leaving the head and tail uncovered. Push the aluminium foil towards the fish. Splash the top salt layer lightly with water to help form a crust when it bakes and seal the parcel carefully.

4. Bake for 20 minutes then let the fish rest for 10 minutes before removing the salt.

5. Crack the salt crust gently with a knife. Remove the top layer of salt. Gently remove the fish to a plate, being careful not to break the skin. Remove the herbs, lemon and any salt remaining on the fish.

WHOLE SALMON COOKED IN SALT

The only problem with big fish like whole salmon is that you might have trouble fitting it into the oven, although baking a whole salmon is the best way to cook it any day. If you want, you can use egg whites, as in the following recipe for whole salmon.

You will need:
- 1 small to medium salmon, about 2.25 kg (5 lb), cleaned
- 6 egg whites
- 8 tbsp cold water
- 3 kg (7 lb) kosher or coarse salt
- 2 tbsp oil

Method:
1. Preheat the oven to 200°C (400°F, gas mark 6).
2. Whisk together the egg whites and enough water to combine with the salt in a large mixing bowl. The salt mixture should hold together when you press it between your hands.
3. Proceed as for the recipe above, using the oil to prepare the foil.
4. Bake for 40 minutes and then rest to continue cooking out of the oven for another 20 minutes.
5. Complete as for the previous recipe.

SALTED COD WITH CREAM

I've often wondered what people do with salted fish I see them buying at the supermarket and local produce market in France where we spend a lot of our time. If you buy salted fish you normally need to soak it in cold water for 12 hours, changing the water every few hours to remove the salt. This recipe may provide the answer, although I still prefer fresh fish, or smoked salmon. Freezing has all but stopped the need for salting, but each to their own.

You will need: Serves 2 to 3
- 500 g (about 1 lb) salt cod   1 tbsp flour
- 150 ml (5 fl oz) water   25 g (1 oz) butter
- 150 ml (5 fl oz) milk   Black pepper

Method:

1. Divide the fish into small fillets, put into a pan with the water and salt, and simmer for about 10—15 minutes. Take the fish out with a slotted spoon and keep warm.

2. Make a roux with the flour and butter and add to the liquid, stirring all the time. Add pepper and serve with the fish.

SALT AND CHEESE-MAKING

Salt is an integral part of the cheese-making process and has served four distinct purposes for centuries.

- It slows down the development of bacteria at the beginning of the process.
- Bacteria help to form the curds and whey and the salt speeds up the expulsion of whey from the curd.
- It prevents the growth of harmful bacteria by preserving it, especially while cheese is maturing.
- It acts as a flavour enhancer. Cheese without salt wouldn't taste very nice and would quickly become unfit to eat.

The salt content is normally shown on the nutritional labelling of most cheeses but is labelled as sodium, as described earlier. This is the sodium content in grams or milligrams per 100 grams of cheese.

With over 400 varieties of British cheese and many hundreds of other cheeses around the world, there is obviously a great range of types and a wide range of salt content. Soft and fresh cheeses contain less salt and a higher moisture content, so have a shorter shelf life. Many continental hard cheeses use brine baths to add the salt and have a higher salt content. I recently bought some hard goat cheese from our supermarket, thinking that as we don't eat a lot of cheese it would keep longer than the softer rolls of goat cheese we eat in France. The shelf life or best before date was three months away and the salt content considerably higher than expected at 1.5 grams per 100 grams of cheese. With so many factors regarding salt content as well as fat content to consider, my only option seems to be to abstain more often!

Comparison of salt content in some typical cheeses
These are given as examples only and the salt content
will vary between brands and fat content. There is a
surprising variation:

Type of cheese	Mg of salt per 100 g cheese
Low-fat fromage frais	36
Full-fat cream cheese	288
Low-fat cream cheese	438
Cottage cheese	300
Wensleydale/Lancashire type	500
Brie	556
Red Leicester	630
Cheddar type	723
Parmesan	756
Stilton (blue)	788
Feta	1440
Roquefort	1670

I was interested to note, while researching, that processed
cheese slices are only just behind feta in their salt content.
Considering that these form a large part of some children's
packed lunches in my experience, there's a lot of salt being
consumed by some young people, even without a packet of
crisps every day. The recommended daily intake is lower for
children than adults, at 2 grams per day for children up to
6 years and 5 grams per day for 7- to 14-year-olds.

MAKING CHEESE

Home-made cheeses have a shelf life of about a week,
if you want to try, and you can decrease the salt content
that way. You can, apparently, use a microwave to save
the need for a double boiler. You need ten times as much
milk as you will make cheese.

SOFT CHEESE

You will need:

3.6 litres (1 gallon) pasteurized milk

1 rennet tablet

50 ml (2 fl oz) cold water

125 ml (4$^1/_2$ fl oz) unsalted buttermilk or 50 ml (2 fl oz) natural (plain) yogurt

3 tsp salt

Method:

1. Put the milk into the upper part of a double boiler with enough water in the bottom to prevent the milk from burning or scorching. Stir in buttermilk or yogurt and warm slowly to 34°C (92° to 94°F). Keep the milk at this temperature for the following steps.

2. Add the rennet tablet dissolved in cold water. Stir into the milk for 2 to 3 minutes. Allow the milk to rest undisturbed for about 30 minutes, until a firm gel forms.

3. To test for curd formation, cut a slit in the curd with a metal spatula and lift it slightly. If the cut in the curd breaks clean, it is ready for the next stage.

4. Cut the curd into cubes. Stir gently and continuously for 20 to 30 minutes to help firm curds whilst keeping the temperature constant.

5. Pour off the whey (liquid) and allow the curds to settle. Add 1 teaspoon salt and mix gently at 5-minute intervals until all the salt is used.

6. Divide the curds into two batches and put into muslin bags or a colander lined with cheesecloth. Squeeze the cheese over the sink to allow excess whey to drain. If you prefer, put the cheese into containers to form a regular shape, still in the cheesecloth and press. Leave a weight on top and leave for 3 or 4 hours.

7. Remove the formed cheese and the cloth. Rewrap tightly in plastic or waxed paper and store in a refrigerator. Use within a week.

MAKING PIZZA CHEESE

You can use half whole milk and half skimmed, or all semi-skimmed for this recipe. I include this for the process as much as anything. I can't think why people buy cheese these days when you can make it so simply! (I gave up on yogurt, making some years ago because of the time it took to get the milk right.)

You will need:
> 3.6 litres (1 gallon) pasteurized milk
> 50 ml (2 fl oz) natural (plain) yogurt
> 1 rennet tablet
> 125 ml (4$^1/_4$ fl oz) cold water
> 1 kg (2 lb) salt dissolved in 3.6 litres (1 gallon) water

Method:
1. Heat the milk to 32°C (90°F) in a double pan and add the yogurt. Stir slowly for 15 minutes while maintaining this constant temperature.
2. Dissolve the rennet in the water and add to the pan, stirring for 3 to 5 minutes.
3. Cover, maintaining the temperature. Allow to stand until coagulated, which will take about 30 minutes.
4. Cut the curd into small cubes. Allow to stand for 15 minutes with occasional stirring.
5. Slowly increase the temperature to 48°C (118°F) over a period of 45 minutes. Hold this temperature for another 15 minutes.
6. Allow the curds and whey to separate. Remove the whey and transfer the curd to a flat pan that can be kept warm. Turn it over every 15 minutes for a 2-hour period without breaking.
7. Cut the curd into long strips, 2–5 cm (1–2 in) wide. Put in hot water at 80°C (180°F). Using wooden spoons, tumble and stretch it underwater until it becomes elastic. This will take about 15 minutes.
8. Remove the curd from hot water and shape it by hand into a ball or a loaf. Place in cold water for about an hour.
9. Remove the cheese from the water and put into the cold salt solution in a plastic bucket or bowl and leave for 24 hours.
10. Remove the cheese from the brine and let it dry for several hours. Wrap in plastic film and refrigerate.

That's all there is to it, apart from making the pizza, that is!

Black salt is an unrefined mineral salt that is actually pinkish grey and has a strong sulphuric flavour. Black salt is mined in India and is used extensively in Indian cuisine as a condiment or added to chaats, chutneys, raitas and many other savoury Indian snacks. Chaat masala, an Indian spice blend, is dependent upon black salt for its characteristic aroma and flavour. Chemically, black salt is almost pure sodium chloride, with iron and trace minerals.

SAUCES AND SEASONINGS

Some cultures don't salt their meals directly but use salty sauces to flavour the dishes. Sodium levels are therefore quite high in foods that include large quantities of soy sauce or other oriental sauces. Our own Worcestershire sauce contains a lot of salt, although there is no indication on the bottle of quantity, and trying to read the amounts on other ketchup and brown sauce bottles isn't easy unless you have a magnifying glass as well as reading glasses!

SOY SAUCE
Soy sauces are made from whole soybeans and wheat, rice or barley grains, but many cheaper brands are made from hydrolyzed soy protein. These latter sauces do not have the natural colour of authentic soy sauces and contain caramel colouring. Traditionally, soy sauces were fermented naturally, in giant urns and under the sun. Nowadays, most of the commercially produced sauces are fermented under factory conditions. Nearly all soy sauce has some alcohol added during bottling to act as a preservative. It should always be kept refrigerated and out of direct sunlight, otherwise it may become bitter.

Soy sauce originated in ancient China and has since been integrated into the traditional cuisines of many East Asian and South-east Asian cultures. Soy sauces produced in different cultures are very different in taste, consistency, fragrance and saltiness. Like olive oils, the quality of the sauce depends on the pressing of the beans. There are two main Chinese varieties:

- Light/fresh soy sauce is thin, opaque and dark brown. It is the main soy sauce used for seasoning, since it is saltier, but it also adds flavour without colouring the food.
- Dark/old soy sauce is slightly thicker, aged longer and contains added molasses to give a distinctive appearance. This type is mainly used during cooking since its flavour develops under heating. It has a richer, slightly sweeter and less salty flavour than light soy sauce.

Thick soy sauce has been thickened with starch and sugar and may also contain monosodium glutamate. You may be interested to know that Worcestershire sauce, made from anchovies, onions and garlic is called 'foreigners' soy sauce' in parts of China and Malaysia.

Japanese soy sauces include wheat as a primary ingredient, and this tends to give them a slightly sweeter, alcoholic, sherry-like taste. Low-salt sauces also exist, but you cannot make soy sauce without salt. On a positive note, a recent study showed that Chinese dark soy sauce contains ten times the antioxidants of red wine. Unfortunately is doesn't contain the benefits of other soy products such as tofu and the salt content may rule it out of the diet anyway. Tests have found that nearly a quarter of soy sauces made from hydrolyzed soy protein contain chemicals with the potential to cause cancer. It is becoming a food allergen for many people, so maybe I'm not the only one with whom it doesn't agree. I'll stick to using balsamic vinegar in my stir-fries, with a drop of sherry if available.

VIETNAMESE COOKING
Fish prepared in a variety of ways is the most common protein in the Vietnamese diet. The most common condiment for steamed, sautéed or fried fish is *nuoc mam* – a fish sauce made from salted and fermented anchovies. The Vietnamese diet can be high in sodium, with its reliance on fish sauce, and low in fibre with its lack of whole grains.

PORRIDGE RECIPES

Having previously prepared a whole book on the benefits of porridge I felt obliged to include some recipes that include salt.

TRADITIONAL SCOTTISH PORRIDGE I

You will need:

1 cup of oatmeal	Knob of butter
3 cups of water	$^1/_2$ tsp salt
1$^1/_2$ cups of milk	

Method:

1. Put oatmeal, water and milk in a pan, stirring all the time.
2. Bring to the boil, add butter and salt.
3. Keep stirring until it thickens.

TRADITIONAL SCOTTISH PORRIDGE II

You will need:

110 g (4 oz) oatmeal
150 ml ($^1/_4$ pt) milk
575 ml (1 pt) boiling water
1 tsp salt

Method:

1. Mix the oatmeal and milk together to form a paste, then add the boiling water.
2. Heat and simmer for 15 minutes, stirring occasionally.
3. Stir in the salt and serve.

BREAD-MAKING

Bread-making is another process that needs salt to control the action of yeast. Making bread in a machine leads to over-rising of the dough if you don't use salt at all and a disappointing end product. You can cut the amount of salt, but don't leave it out altogether. If you use bicarbonate of soda as a raising agent instead of yeast you are still using a fair amount of sodium. Here are some fairly healthy bread recipes. Being home made, at least you'll have the satisfaction of knowing exactly what's in it.

WHOLEMEAL BREAD

You don't have to invest in a bread-maker or a lot of equipment to enjoy home-made bread. I used to make a lot of it and often used cake tins to make round dome-shaped loaves.

You will need:

1.5 kg (3 lb) wholemeal (whole-wheat) flour
1 tbsp salt
25 g (1 oz) fresh yeast or 1 sachet dried yeast and 2 tbsp warm water

50 g (2 oz) fine oatmeal
1 litre (35 fl oz) warm water
2 tbsp malt extract
2 tbsp oil

Method:
1. Mix together the flour, oatmeal and salt in a large bowl.
2. Mix the yeast with some of the water and leave to froth.
3. Add the flour and the rest of the water, malt and oil. Mix to a smooth dough.
4. Knead on a floured board for about 10 minutes until elastic. Put into a clean bowl, cover and leave in a warm place for a couple of hours, until it has doubled in size.
5. Preheat the oven to 220°C (425°F, gas mark 5) and grease four x 500 g (1 lb) loaf tins. Alternatively, use cake tins and make round loaves.
6. Turn the dough on to a floured board again. Knead a little then divide into four. Shape and place in the tins, sprinkling a few oats or sesame or poppy seeds on top (optional). Leave for about 20 minutes and bake for

15 minutes. Lower the temperature to 190°C (375°F, gas mark 5) and bake for a further 20–25 minutes. When done, the loaves should sound hollow when tapped.
7. Cool on a wire rack.

OAT ROLLS

You will need:

25 g (1 oz) fresh yeast or 1 sachet dried yeast and 2 tbsp warm water
1 tbsp honey
1 tsp salt

425 ml ($^3/_4$ pt) skimmed milk
225 g (8 oz) oatmeal
450 g (1 lb) wholemeal (whole-wheat) or plain (all-purpose) flour

Method:

1. Mix the yeast with the honey. Warm the milk and stir in the oatmeal. Add the yeast to the oats and leave to stand for an hour.
2. Stir in the flour and salt and knead to form a dough. It should be soft but not too dry. Leave to rest for 30 minutes.
3. Knead again for a couple of minutes. Don't be heavy handed.
4. Divide into 12 portions and make into balls. Make a dent in the centre of each one.
5. Leave to rise for another 30 minutes on a greased baking tray and preheat the oven to 220°C (425°F, gas mark 7).
6. Bake for 15–20 minutes until the rolls sound hollow when knocked. Cool on a rack.

SODA BREAD

This is the easiest bread to make. It uses buttermilk which gives a distinctive flavour. If, like me, you have trouble getting hold of buttermilk, you can make the milk sour with the addition of lemon juice.

You will need:

250 g (9 oz) plain (all-purpose) flour
250 g (9 oz) wholemeal (whole-wheat) flour
2 tsp bicarbonate of soda
$^1/_2$ tsp salt

25 g (1 oz) butter, cut in pieces
450ml (16 fl oz) buttermilk or semi-skimmed milk
Juice of a lemon (if using milk)

Method:
1. Preheat the oven to 220°C (425°F, gas mark 7) and dust a baking sheet with flour.
2. If using milk, pour it into a jug and add the lemon juice. Leave to stand for 15 minutes.
3. Sift the white flour, salt and bicarbonate of soda into a large bowl and add the wholemeal flour.
4. Rub in the butter. Make a well in the centre and gradually pour in the buttermilk or milk. Combine from the centre with a wooden spoon or your fingers, handling it gently. The dough should be soft but not sloppy. If it gets too wet add a little more flour.
5. Turn on to a floured board and shape it into a flat, round loaf, about 5cm (2in) thick.
6. Put the loaf on to the baking sheet and score a deep cross in the top with a floured knife. Bake for 20–25 minutes until the bottom of the loaf sounds hollow when tapped. Reduce the heat to 190°C (375°F, gas mark 5) and cook for a further 25 minutes, or until the crust is browned.
7. Transfer to a wire rack and eat while still warm.

PRESERVED FRUIT AND VEGETABLES

In Victorian times salt was still used widely to preserve food, along with copious amounts of sugar, vinegar and ice saved from winter weather, if Mrs Beeton is anything to go by. I've just seen a recipe for mango chutney, using 50 green mangoes and a pound of salt, 3 pounds of sugar and 6 pints of vinegar, but I'm giving it a wide berth. What about cockles, covered in vinegar, peppercorns and salt? Not for me, thanks.

Here are just a few common and/or quirky ways to preserve with salt. I'll leave you to decide.

I remember how, when first married and with a garden of runner beans, I decided to salt some of them. We didn't have a freezer back in the dark ages, 30 odd years ago.

I spent ages stringing and slicing them to pack into a wine maker's demi-john (I was into the whole thing, including elderberry wine). The result was a disappointing, grey, salty mass of beans which wouldn't come out of the jar very easily. We got a freezer soon after that!

PRESERVED CUCUMBERS

You will need:

Salt and cucumbers

Method:
1. Peel and thinly slice the cucumbers. Sprinkle liberally with salt and leave for 24 hours.
2. Drain off the liquid and pack into clean jars, sprinkling each layer with more salt. Cover with a non-metallic lid.
3. To use, wash well in cold water. Drain and dress with pepper, vinegar and oil. Obviously, no salt needed!

SALTED ALMONDS

You will need:

225 g (8 oz) blanched, whole almonds
150 ml (5 fl oz) vegetable oil
1 tbsp celery salt
$1/4$ tsp cayenne pepper

Method:
1. Fry the almonds in the oil until brown. Drain on kitchen paper.
2. Toss in the celery salt and pepper. Serve in small fancy paper cases.

SALTED PEANUTS

You may be interested to know that peanuts can be salted in their shells simply by soaking them in brine before drying them by roasting. This leaves a salt residue behind on the nut in the shell. Sometimes a vacuum is used to remove air from the batch before the brine is introduced.

PRESERVED LEMONS

This Middle Eastern method of preserving lemons can be used with a variety of dishes such as stews and rice dishes, added at the end of the cooking.

You will need:
  8 unwaxed lemons
  4 tbsp coarse sea salt

Method:
1. Cut four of the lemons into quarters. Smother in sea salt and squash into a preserving jar. Cover and leave for two or three days.
2. Juice the remaining lemons and add to the jar. Leave for four weeks.
3. To use, scoop out the flesh and add the peel to the dish.

SALT AND ALCOHOL

PEPPER AND VODKA-SOAKED CHERRY TOMATOES

There's nothing like something salty to eat with a drink before dinner. This could dispense with the need for the drink and save time as an all-in-one treat!

You will need: **Serves 6**
  250 g (9 oz) baby plum or cherry tomatoes, stalks removed
  200 ml (7 fl oz) vodka
  1 tbsp sherry
  1 tbsp Worcestershire sauce
  Drops of Tabasco sauce
  $1/2$ tsp celery salt

You will need for the dip:
  1 tsp celery salt
  $1/4$ tsp cayenne pepper
  2 tbsp sea salt

Method:

1. Score a cross in each tomato base, as if you are preparing brussels sprouts.
2. Mix together the vodka, sherry, Worcestershire sauce and celery salt. Add a few drops of Tabasco. Pour over the tomatoes and leave to marinate for at least 24 hours, covered, in the refrigerator.
3. Drain the tomatoes and serve at room temperature. Keep the marinade for other batches, or dispose of how you wish . . .
4. Mix the dipping spices together. Arrange the tomatoes around the dip and enjoy. Cheers.

TEQUILA SHOTS

The Mexican drink known as tequila derives from a fermented drink the Aztec people made from the agave plant, long before the Spanish conquistadors arrived in 1521. When the Spanish ran out of brandy, they began to distill this agave drink.

One, two three, floor!

The modern way to drink tequila is a communal event, with everyone downing their drink together. A single shot of tequila is often served with a pinch of salt and a slice of lemon or lime. This is called 'tequila cruda'. The drinker licks the back of their hand below the index finger and pours on the salt. The salt is licked off the hand, tequila is drunk and the fruit slice is quickly bitten. What fun! The salt lessens the burn of the tequila and the citrus juice is said to enhance the flavour.

Mexican people have long known that a little salt on the tongue can help to mollify the fiery flavour of much of their food — chilli peppers, for instance. By the same token, citrus juices of various kinds have long been used to kill the aftertaste of more potent forms of alcohol. Try the following recipe for a chaser.

SANGRITA CHASER

This a spicy and refreshing non-alcoholic chaser made of fresh orange juice, grenadine and chilli piquín or a mix of different chillies. Sangrita owes its name to the Spanish diminutive for 'blood'. Commercially bottled brands are available, but you can make your own.

You will need:
> 1 litre (35 fl oz)freshly squeezed orange juice
> 150—300 ml (5—10 fl oz) fresh lime juice
> 1 tbsp grenadine syrup
> 1 tbsp salt
> $1/4$ tbsp Chilli piquín (optional) or few drops
>> Tabasco sauce

If you want really red sangrita you can add tomato juice as well.

Method:
Mix all of the ingredients together and drink a shot of tequila, followed by a glass of sangrita.

GOLDEN HONEY MARGARITA

If you are too old for the whole tequila shot business, like me, you might prefer this drink.

You will need for each drink:
> 1 part tequila
> $1/2$ shot Triple Sec/Cointreau
> 1 part honey syrup
> 2 parts lemon juice
> Salt

Method:
1. Shake all the ingredients together except the salt, with ice.
2. Strain into a large cocktail glass with a salted rim.

SWEET AND SALTY FOOD

Whilst at an asparagus festival in France recently, I noticed, among the local produce, a number of pots of jam, preserves and some caramel spread made with sea salt. I declined the offer to purchase some, but was not that surprised to see salt included in a sweet spread. As proof that a number of sweet recipes contain salt, here is a biscuit recipe guaranteed to contain 7 per cent salt: not to be recommended on health grounds. I even found one aptly called 'Cookies of death'.

CHOC CHIP AND SALT COOKIES

You will need:
- 120 g (4 oz) soft butter
- 200 g (7 oz) brown sugar
- 2 tbsp white sugar
- 1 egg, beaten
- 1 tsp vanilla extract
- 1$\frac{1}{2}$ tsp instant coffee
- 225 g (8 oz) flour
- $\frac{1}{2}$ tsp bicarbonate of soda
- $\frac{1}{2}$ tsp baking powder
- $\frac{1}{2}$ tsp salt
- 200 g (7 oz) chocolate chips
- 50 g (2 oz) chopped nuts

Method:
1. Preheat oven to 140°C (275°F, gas mark 1).
2. Cream together the butter and sugars. Add the egg, vanilla and coffee. Beat well.
3. Fold in the flour, salt, baking powder and bicarbonate of soda. Add the choc chips and nuts, mixing gently.
4. Form into balls of the desired size. Place on greased baking sheets with room to spread.
5. Bake for 20–25 minutes and allow to cool for 10 minutes before taking them off the sheets, when they will harden.

Hints
& Tips

There are many ways in which salt can be used around the home. Don't just look upon salt as a seasoning that should be used sparingly. Here are a few suggestions for helping with some tough domestic jobs. Many of these may look slightly familiar, especially if you have read a book on the benefits of bicarbonate of soda recently. I have tried not to overlap too much, although bicarbonate of soda can be used to perhaps greater effect in many cases. You may, of course, as always, take some of them with a pinch of . . . sodium chloride.

FOOD-RELATED USES

DESCALING FISH
Soak fish in salt water before removing the scales, which will come off more easily.

FISHY NIFFS
Can you still smell the fish? Dip a lemon wedge in salt and rub the item (hands, cutting board, or work surface) before rinsing with water.

FREE-FLOWING SALT
Add a few grains of rice to the salt cellar to keep the salt flowing freely.

CLEANING LETTUCE
Adding salt to the water will get rid of unwanted insects and slugs. If it doesn't get rid of them all, at least they'll be dead.

TEST FOR FRESHNESS OF EGGS
Put an egg into a cup of salt water. If it floats, ditch it.

CRACKING EGGS!
If you want to boil a cracked egg, or prevent one from spoiling if it cracks in the water, add some salt to the pan to keep the egg in the shell.

FLUFFY EGG WHITES
Adding a pinch of salt to egg whites helps to make them fluffier when beating.

CRACKING NUTS
Soak whole, unshelled nuts in brine overnight. They will crack out of their shells whole when you tap the end with a hammer.

PREVENT FOOD FROM STICKING
Rub salt on to a griddle to prevent food from sticking.

REVIVING JADED APPLES
I hope they don't do this in shops. Wrinkled apples can be soaked in mild salt solution to perk them up. Fruits put in mildly salted water after peeling will not discolour. The same applies to lemon juice. On the other hand, if you use too much salt you could end up with a mummified apple. See the chapter on Fascinating Facts.

Salt is also said to improve the taste of cooking apples.

REDUCING SALT CONTENT
Add raw potatoes to stews and soups that are too salty. Don't eat them, of course.

SETTING GELATINE
Gelatine sets more quickly when a dash of salt is added to it.

MOPPING UP IN THE OVEN
If something bubbles over in your oven, put a handful of salt on top of the spilled juice. The mess won't smell and will bake into a dry, light crust which you can wipe off easily when the oven has cooled.

You can also sprinkle salt into milk-scorched pans to remove the odour.

CLEANING A COFFEE POT OR JUG
Use salt to clean your discoloured coffee pot or jug.

CLEANING USES

These tips are passed on in good faith. If in doubt about cleaning a particular item, please refer to expert advice.

BATH AND TOILET CLEANER
Some people must have very grubby baths, or very grubby bodies. Mixing salt with turpentine whitens your bathtub and toilet bowl, apparently. Not recommended for smokers!

REMOVING GREASE
To remove grease stains on clothing, mix one part salt to four parts alcohol. If it works on the bath, it will work on the clothes.

PRESERVING BRUSHES
Soak new brushes in warm, salty water before you first use them. They will apparently last longer.

DISCOLOURED GLASS
Soak discoloured glass in a salt and vinegar solution to remove stains.

STOCKINGS OR TIGHTS
If you have odd stockings or tights of different colours try boiling them in salty water and they will come out matched, and hopefully without holes.

HANDKERCHIEF STAIN REMOVAL
If you are the type who still prefers to use real handkerchiefs, especially when you have a cold (they don't seem to hurt the tender bits when you have a very runny nose), soak them in salt water before washing. You can then rinse them before washing alongside other clothes in the washing machine.

REMOVING INK FROM A CARPET
To remove an ink spot from a carpet, pour salt on to the stain and let it soak up the liquid before brushing up the salt. As with all stain removal, try on an inconspicuous bit of carpet first.

BLOODSTAINS
Nosebleed? Cut finger? Soak clothing in a bucket of salty water as soon as possible to prevent staining.

PRESERVING CLOTHES PINS
Boiling clothes pins in salt water before using them may make them last longer, apparently. They'll need careful drying, however.

METAL CLEANER
Clean brass, copper and pewter with a paste made from salt and vinegar, thickened with flour. Bicarbonate of soda works better I think, and without the flour.

NEW LAMPS FOR OLD
Polish your old kerosene lamp with salt for a brighter look. You never know what genie you may find!

REMOVING RED WINE FROM A TABLECLOTH
Since you can't usually whip off the tablecloth if a guest spills red wine on your best cloth, just pour a little salt on to the splash immediately. This will soak up the wine and then you can soak the cloth at the end of the meal and brush up any salt that has escaped the cloth.

REFRESHING WHITES
Restore yellowed cottons or linens to their original white by boiling the items for one hour in a salt and bicarbonate of soda solution. Perspiration stains may be removed by adding four tablespoons of salt to a litre (2 pints) of hot water. If you can't soak the item, sponge the fabric with the solution until the stains disappear.

CLEANING AN IRON
Rub some salt on to a damp cloth and apply to a warm, but not hot, iron. Switch off the iron first, of course.

CLEANING A PIANO
I'm not brave enough to subject our ancient piano keys to this one, I'm afraid. Perhaps it is better for newer models rather than ivory. The suggestion is to mix lemon juice with salt to clean the keys.

GETTING RID OF SOAP SUDS
Rinsing clothes with a little salt in the water can get rid of excess soap. This is also said to allow fabrics to hold their colour.

CLOTHES LINES
This is a bit tricky with a rotary clothes line, but soaking your clothes line in salt water will prevent your clothes from freezing to the line. Alternatively, use salt in your final rinse to prevent the clothes from freezing. Better still, dry them indoors.

CLEANING PANS
Soak enamelled pans in salt water overnight and boil them with salty water the next day to remove burned-on stains. Don't soak chipped pans or metal ones.

WICKER FURNITURE
Rub any wicker furniture you may have with salt water to prevent yellowing.

CLEANING CLOTHS AND SPONGES
Freshen sponges and cloths by soaking them in salt water.

RINGS ON FURNITURE
Remove white rings left on tables caused by wet or hot dishes and glasses. Rub a thin paste of salad oil and salt on to the spot and let the mixture stand for an hour or two before removing. As always, try out the technique first on a less conspicuous mark if possible. Complete the process by polishing the whole item of furniture.

PEST PREVENTION

ANT DETERRENT
Sprinkle salt on to your shelves to keep ants away. I don't recommend this where you may have any damp getting in, or where the salt is likely to spill on to a floor.

WEEDS AND SLUGS
Use salt for killing weeds in your lawn or slugs and snails in the garden.

WEED-FREE PATHS

Sprinkle salt between bricks or paving slabs where you don't want grass (or any other plants) to grow.

MISCELLANEOUS

FLOWERS

Add a pinch of salt to the water in the vase your cut flowers will stand in. They will last longer.

VASES

Clean the grot and nasty smell out of vases after the flowers are dead by rubbing the inside with salt water.

CANDLES

Soak new candles in a strong salt solution for a few hours and then dry to reduce dripping wax.

WINDOWS

To keep single-glazed windows from freezing outside, rub the inside of the window with a sponge dipped in a salt water solution and wipe dry.

PERSONAL CARE

SORE MOUTHS

Mild salt water makes an effective mouthwash. Use it hot for a sore throat gargle.

BRUSHING TEETH

Use equal parts of salt and bicarbonate of soda for brushing your teeth. Dry salt sprinkled on your toothbrush makes a good tooth polisher. Ouch!

CUTS AND SCRATCHES

A mild salt solution is a good way to clean small cuts and scratches, using the antibacterial qualities of salt.

REMOVING A SPLINTER

To remove a splinter from a finger easily, soak the area in warm salty water for a few minutes. If this doesn't work, mix a little water with half a teaspoon of bicarbonate of soda to form a paste. Apply this to a splinter and cover it with a plaster for a couple of hours. The soda should draw out the splinter, which can then be easily removed, along with any toxins, and solve the problem.

FACIAL
For a stimulating facial, mix equal parts of sea salt and olive oil. Gently massage in with long upward strokes. Remove and wash with mild soap and warm water.

HAIR RINSE
Mix one part bicarbonate of soda to two parts water to form a paste. Massage into the scalp and it will cleanse your hair of shampoo and product build-up. Rinse well with warm water.

BATH TREATMENTS

Bath treatments can be used to help a wide range of ailments and to help you relax. If you can't run away to a spa or afford a pricey treatment, try one of these. Don't fill the bath too full so you can add more hot water when required. If you can't run to a whole bath try soaking your feet instead. It will revive you in no time.

BATH SOAK
Sea salt can be used for a hot soak. Try adding a cup of sea salt to a bath and soaking for at least ten minutes. You will feel soothed and clean. Add a few drops of your favourite scented oils to soften the skin.

BATH DETOX
Use one part (3 tablespoons) bicarbonate of soda to one part sea salt in a hot bath. Lie back and relax for 20 minutes. Rinse off or shower to remove the salt. For a more luxurious soak, add a tablespoon of citric acid and a few drops of essential oil to the salt and bicarbonate of soda.

You can mix up a jarful and add food colouring as well for a gift idea.

SPORT-RELIEF SOAK

Mmm, smell that wintergreen . . .

You will need:
   1 cup coarse sea salt
   2 drops of wintergreen essential oil
   2 drops of eucalyptus essential oil
   1 drop of peppermint essential oil

Method:
Just add all the ingredients together and mix well.

BODY SCRUB

Very thorough, for real toughies.

You will need:
   $1/2$ cup coarse sea salt
   $1/4$ cup rosemary oil

Method:
Put some oil on a loofah then dip it into the salt. Using circular movements, rub over the skin. Give extra attention to rough areas. Continue to do this until your body is covered. Rinse with a warm water shower and pat dry. Follow up with moisturizer.

COFFEE AND GRAPEFRUIT THIGH SCRUB

This makes two applications, if you can bare it! It will keep in an airtight container until you forget what it was like the first time. Coffee stimulates fatty congestion and grapefruit stimulates the lymphatic system, removing toxins from the body.

You will need:

$1/2$ cup sea salt	10 drops peppermint oil
$1/4$ cup clay	15 drops grapefruit essential oil
1 tsp ground coffee	15 drops orange essential oil
1 tsp cinnamon	

Method:
Combine all the ingredients together, breaking up any clumps. To use mix 2 tablespoons with enough water or milk to form a smooth paste. Massage into the thigh and buttock areas. Rinse off in the shower.

Fascinating Facts

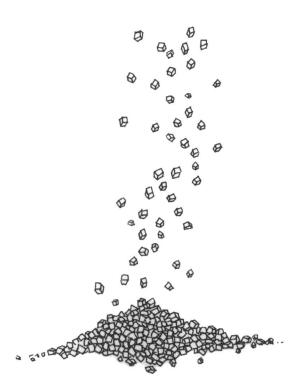

THE LANGUAGE OF SALT

SALTY WORDS
Roman soldiers were paid for some of their service in salt. This is where we get the word salary from. Also from Roman times we get the word salacious. Gossip of a salty kind is today referred to as 'appealing to or stimulating sexual desire, lascivious'. The Romans liked a good gossip over affairs of the heart, apparently, as much as the next man or woman.

WORTH HIS SALT?
There is more than one possible derivation of this phrase. Some say that it refers to the days when salt was a very precious commodity. Since Roman soldiers were paid partly in salt, it became equated with wages. A person not worth his salt did not, therefore, give value for money. Others would have it that the phrase originated in ancient Greece, where slaves were traded for salt. An unruly slave was not worth his salt.

PINCH OF SALT, ANYONE?
The phrase today suggests scepticism, caution or incredulity. One suggestion is that salt makes things more flavoursome, so easier to swallow. The Roman phrase *cum grano salis*, meaning 'with a grain of salt', seems to come from the Roman historian Pliny the Elder, who wrote that the general Pompey had discovered an antidote for poison that was to be taken *cum grano salis*. This was apparently to make the antidote more effective. Other etymologists believe that Pliny had been sceptical about the antidote and, therefore, took the phrase to mean 'with a dose of scepticism'. Believe what you will.

SALTY ADDITIVES
Sauce, salami, salad, sausage and salsa also come from the word for salt, because they all require salt in their making or preparation to give a unique flavour.

EATING SALT TOGETHER
In Greek, Roman and Semitic cultures, 'eating or taking salt' with a person forged a sacred bond of hospitality. Salt has been used in rituals since ancient times. The devil

is said to hate salt, which is why it has been used in holy water and placed on the tongues of infants at baptism.

SYMBOL OF PURITY
Salt is a symbol of purity and incorruptibility. In Numbers 18:19, 'a covenant of salt' means a covenant that cannot be broken. Jesus says to his followers, in Matthew 5:13, 'Ye are the salt of the earth'.

ABOVE OR BELOW THE SALT
In the days of knights and banquet halls your position at the table was shown by the proximity of the 'saler' or salt cellar (see below) and signified a place of esteem if you sat 'above the salt'. This meant that you were in a position of honour, close to the head of the household. Equally, it meant that you sat, as a visiting noble, with the grown-up members of the family and other important members of the household. Minor officials, subordinates and others sat below. All a bit 'upstairs downstairs', really.

HELLO SALER
The 'cellar' part of salt cellar comes from the Norman *saler*, itself from the Latin *sal*, meaning 'salt'. Early in the 13th century, the word *celer* meant 'a container for salt'. The original, between salt and *celer*, was forgotten and the word became *salte-seler* in the 15th century, i.e. a salt cellar for salt. The Latin *cellarium*, meaning a 'seat of cells' or a receptacle for food, later replaced *celer*, so that's why a salt receptacle is called a salt cellar. Sounds a bit like 'Call my Bluff', doesn't it?

OLD SALT
This term refers to a sailor, presumably because of his weather-beaten appearance after being exposed to salt, sun, wind and rain over many voyages. Still, better an old salt than a jack tar, gob or a sea dog, which are other endearing names for sailors.

SALTY DOG
A Salty Dog is a cocktail of vodka or gin and grapefruit juice, served in a glass with a salted rim. The salt makes the difference. A Greyhound is the same drink without the salt rim.

FASCINATING FACTS ABOUT SAL

WHAT'S IN A NAME?
You can tell a lot about a place by its name. Place names with Hall, Halle or Sal in them probably developed because of salt deposits or brine springs nearby.

SALZBURG
Salzburg means salt town. The nearby Dürnberg mine was originally worked by the Celts over 2,500 years ago. Salt beds range from a metre to hundreds of metres thick. Salt brought riches to Salzburg, in Austria, in a time when salt was still 'white gold'. Today you can visit the mines and experience them via a cross between a museum and an amusement fair.

THE HALLSTATT 'MAN IN SALT'
The prehistoric 'Man in Salt' was discovered in an old salt mine in Hallstatt, Austria, in 1734. The corpse was discovered preserved in salt 'pressed flat and tightly grown into the rock', with strange clothing and tools. Hallstatt enjoys the title of 'World's oldest salt mine', dating back 7,000 years.

THE ROYAL SALTWORKS OF CHAUX
These salt works at Chaux, in France, constitute a historical monument of worldwide heritage, recognized by UNESCO. Over the last 60 years they have been restored as a testimony to neoclassical architecture. What is more surprising is that the design was applied to industrial buildings, dating from the Age of Enlightenment. Built between 1775 and 1779, the Royal Saltworks used the wood from the Forest of Chaux as firewood, to extract the salt from the water. The water was carried in from the old salt mine of Salins les Bains. Designed by Claude-Nicolas Ledoux, it included 11 buildings in a semi-circle, five of which were workshops and workers' living quarters. Unfortunately for Ledoux, he was imprisoned during the French Revolution and his big plan for a whole 'Ideal City' was never built. The Royal Saltworks closed in 1895 and fell into ruins.

HOW SALTY IS THE SEA?

Sodium chloride is by far the greatest solid present in sea water. Each gallon (4 litres) contains, on average, 105 g (0.23 lb) of salt. Some scientists have estimated that if all the oceans in the world dried up they would produce $14\frac{1}{2}$ times the bulk of the continent of Europe. How would anybody be able to tell if they were right? Should we take this with a mountain of salt?

HALITE

Hopper crystals

Although most crystals of salt are arranged in isometric form, with three axes of symmetry, halite crystals called 'hopper crystals' are sometimes found. These look like skeleton cubes, with the edges extending outward, leaving hollow, stair-step faces between these edges. They form in this way due to different growing rates of the edges and faces from the centres. Some entrepreneurial spirits have started growing these crystals, which form quickly, by putting sticks, animal skulls and other artefacts into lakes for crystals to form. They can then be retrieved, covered in crystals, for sale.

Veined crystals

Purple fibrous halite is found in France. These crystalline specimens can be impressive. The colours reflect the bacterial debris trapped in evaporated lakes. They are highly prized by collectors.

Flowers

Halite flowers are rare stalactites found growing down from the roofs of arid caves under the Nullarbor Plain, in Australia. Halite stalactites have also been found in Michigan. Halite rock is usually 95—99 per cent pure, but is found with gypsum, dolomite, quartz, anhydrite and pyrite.

DEAD BUOYANT

The Dead Sea has such a high concentration of salts that objects which are not usually able to float are buoyant in it. It is impossible to swim on your front in the Dead Sea or to dive without weights. All you need to do is float on your back.

JACK TAR OR BLACK SEA?

One of the most unusual properties of the Dead Sea is the way it discharges asphalt. The Dead Sea constantly spits up small pebbles of the black substance from deep below the water. After earthquakes, chunks as large as houses have been produced.

SALTY REMAINS IN IRAN

In 1993 miners discovered human remains at a salt mine in north-west Iran. The body was buried under a 2-ton rock. Several items, such as a leather sack full of salt, a clay tallow burner, two pairs of leather shoes and two cow horns, were discovered nearby. This was the third set of remains to have been discovered. The items were in considerably good shape, unlike the crushed skeleton.

The second discovery, in 2004, which came to be known as The Salt Man, was the body of a miner preserved by the salt. He lived around 1,700 years ago, but was mummified naturally where he died, complete with long white hair and beard. Aged about 35 years, no mean age in those days, he was wearing leather boots and had some tools and a walnut with him when found. He now resides in the National Museum in Tehran.

Since these discoveries, there seems to have been a lot of activity in 2005, resulting in still more finds. While bulldozing salt into trucks, the Twin Salt Man was unearthed, complete with hair and nails. Some pieces of clothing and a hand-woven thatch rug with a unique texture were discovered with the man, who was 180—185 cm (71—73 in) tall and also aged between 35 and 40.

Another, younger man was found and said to be the most intact of all four found so far. Experts found an iron dagger and scabbard attached to his waist and two ceramic jugs with oil inside: probably used as a lantern. He wore a long quilted item of clothing and gaiters as well as two earrings of indistinguishable material.
The fifth salt man to be found was discovered in Chehr-Abad Mine in Zanjan City. It now seems likely that a large number of men were buried there. The mine was in use from about 400 BC to AD 650. These salt men are among

rare discoveries around the world, mummified as a result of natural conditions. Most of their tissues are well preserved and the conditions in the mines mitigated the effects of micro-organisms.

SALT MINES AND STORAGE
During World War IIo the Third Reich stored paintings, art works and huge amounts of money in salt mines. Today, old salt mines provide storage for petroleum, chemical waste and nuclear waste.

TOO LITTLE SALT
During Napoleon's retreat from Moscow thousands of troops died due to inadequate wound healing and lowered resistance to disease. This was because they were suffering from salt deficiency.

WHAT A WASTE
In January 2007, a competition was held by a radio station in Sacramento, to see who could drink the most water without needing to go to the loo. A Nintendo Wii was the prize, obviously considered a very funny line by the station, until one of the contestants, a 28-year-old mother of three, died from water intoxication. Known as hyponatremia, the condition is usually seen among athletes who consume too much water quickly, causing a critical loss of sodium.

NOW YOU SEA IT!
The Salton Sea is a relative newcomer to southern California and was created by accident 100 years ago, when flooding on the Colorado River allowed water to crash through canal barriers. For the next 18 months the entire flow of the Colorado River rushed downhill into the Salton Trough. Previously this had been the bottom of a dry lake. During earlier geological periods a large body of water had occupied the basin. By the time engineers were finally able to stop the breaching water in 1907, the Salton Sea had been born. Now 72 km (45 miles) long and 32 km (20 miles) wide, this 932 sq km (360 sq mile) basin is a popular site for boaters, water-skiers and anglers. Kayakers, birdwatchers and visitors enjoy the site's many recreation opportunities. Thanks to the sea's low altitude

(69 m/227 ft below sea level), atmospheric pressure improves speed and ski boat engine performance, which is nice . . . unless you're an angler or a swimmer.

WIELICZKA SALT MINE

The Wieliczka Salt Mine is situated outside Krakow and has been worked for 900 years. In medieval times it was one of the world's biggest and most profitable industrial sites, when common salt was the commercial equivalent of oil. Today it is a major tourist attraction with 200 km (124 miles) of passageways and over 2,000 caverns. You can walk underground for about 2,000 m (6,561 ft) in the oldest part of the salt mine and see its subterranean museum, the biggest mining museum in the world.

At a depth of 210 m (689 ft) there is a sanatorium for those suffering from asthma and allergy. Concerts and other events take place in the mine's biggest chambers and the mine has been a UNESCO World Heritage Site since 1978. Beneath the mine there are a number of chapels and churches. Near the entrance is the chapel of Saint Antonius, but, due to the location, the moist air has destroyed the chapel figures. One late 19th-century American traveller described these in amusing terms:

"Here was the chapel of St. Anthony, the oldest in the mines — a Byzantine excavation, supported by columns with altar, crucifix, and life-size statues of saints, apparently in black marble, but all as salt as Lot's wife, as I discovered by putting my tongue to the nose of John the Baptist. The humid air of this upper story of the mines has damaged some of the saints: Francis, especially, is running away like a dip candle, and all of his head is gone except his chin. The limbs of Joseph are dropping off as if he had the Norwegian leprosy, and Lawrence has deeper scars than his gridiron could have made, running up and down his back. A Bengal light, burnt at the altar, brought into sudden life this strange temple, which presently vanished into utter darkness, as if it had never been."

Today they have been described as either more like modern art, or prehistoric sculptures. Other churches, like the cathedral, are well preserved. Here, even the chandeliers are made of salt. The walls are covered with sculptures of saints and scenes from the Bible. Here, the temperature stays at a uniform 15°C (59°F) throughout the year.

One well-travelled Frenchman observed in the 18th century that the Wieliczka Salt Mine was no less magnificent than the Egyptian pyramids. Another described a hall carved like a Greek theatre. There was also a large salt ballroom:

> "... with well-executed statues of Vulcan and Neptune. Six large chandeliers, apparently of cut-glass, but really of salt, illuminate it on festive occasions, and hundreds of dancers perspire themselves into a pretty pickle. I purchased a salt-cellar, which has the property of furnishing salt when it is empty. But it seemed to me that I should not need to use it for some days. I felt myself so thoroughly impregnated with salt, that I conceived the idea of seasoning my soup by stirring it with my fingers, and half-expected that the fresh roast would turn to corned beef in my mouth."
>
> Eva March Tappan

THE SALT CATHEDRAL OF ZIPAQUIRÁ

Underground salt cathedrals are not confined to Europe. This cathedral, near the town of Zipaquirá, in Colombia, South America, was built inside a mountain after exploitation of the salt mines, long before the Spanish conquests. The salt deposits formed 200 million years ago and were raised above sea level when the Andes Mountains were formed in the late Tertiary period.

The miners had carved an earlier sanctuary, but the construction of a modern, subterranean, Roman Catholic church began in the 1950s. Because it was carved into an existing mine, structural problems developed and it was shut down in 1990.

The current cathedral was started in 1991, 61 m (200 ft) below the old one, and was dedicated in 1995. It has 14 small chapels representing the stations of the cross, depicting Jesus's last journey, and the bottom section has three sections, representing the birth, life and death of Jesus.

INCA SALT MINES, MARAS

Visitors to Peru can visit salt works where local people still work the grey-green salt pools layering the hillside, as they have since the days of the Inca kingdom. Every year the rainy season dissolves the hillside and the entire labyrinth of salt pans needs to be rebuilt. For centuries people have directed the brine coming out of the ground to evaporation pools. This salt is then treated and sold in the local market. The sight of the group of about 3,000 pools has been described by tourists as spectacular. Local people show their ancient techniques to the visitors and allow them to participate in the collecting as well as in Andean rites and celebrations. It's a pity they have to do it for tourists.

THE PATIO PROCESS

No, this isn't about using salt to lay slabs on, but about Spanish silver miners in the mid-16th century. It was used to extract silver from silver sulphide ores. Developed in Mexico in 1557, it was the first process to use mercury to recover silver from ore. Silver ores were crushed to a fine slime which was mixed with salt, water, copper sulphate and mercury. It was then spread in a thick layer in a shallow-walled, open enclosure, or patio. Horses were driven around on it to mix it further. After weeks of mixing and soaking in the sun, a reaction converted the silver to metal, which amalgamated with the mercury and was then recovered.

I didn't find out what happened to the horses, but I suspect they needed replacing quite often. But never mind, the patio process solved a crisis in the silver-mining districts of the Spanish colonies. So the colonials were able to keep up the exploitation and continued silver mining for centuries in Mexico, Peru and Bolivia.